Fulfillment of Promises

Deborah Bigler

This book or parts thereof may not be reproduced in any form, stored in a retrieval system, or transmitted in any form by any means, be it electronic, mechanical, photocopy, recording, or otherwise without prior written permission of the publisher, except as proved by United States of America copyright law.

All scriptures have been taken directly from Bible Hub. © 2004 - 2025 by Bible Hub Biblehub.com

The World English Bible (WEB) is a 1997 revision of the American Standard Version of the Holy Bible, first published in 1901. It is in the Public Domain. Please feel free to copy and distribute it freely. Thank you to Michael Paul Johnson for making this work available. For the latest information, to report corrections, or for other correspondence, visit www.ebible.org. All rights preserved.

New Heart English Bible (NHEB). Edited by Wayne A. Mitchell. Public Domain 2008-2025 All rights preserved.

Copyright © 2025 Deborah Bigler
All rights reserved.

ISBN 13: 979-8-9911733-4-6

While the author has made every effort to provide accurate internet addresses at the time of publication, neither the publisher nor the author assumes any responsibility for errors or for changes that occur after publication. Further, the publisher does not have any control over and does not assume any responsibility for author or third-party websites or their contents.

Printed in the United States.

Table of Contents

1. All of the Promises Given to Israel Fulfilled
    a. Millennial Kingdom --------------------------------- 2
    b. Jerusalem, City of God ------------------------- 13
    c. Celebration of the Feast of Tabernacles   29
    d. Temple of God, His Presence in the Land of Israel -- 35
    e. God's Glory Returns to the Temple --------- 52
    f. Healing Water of God That Flows From the Temple -- 57
    g. The Great Altar Restored ----------------------- 61
    h. The Priesthood Restored ----------------------- 64
    i. Inheritance of the Land of Israel ------------ 85
    j. End of the Thousand Years and Judgment of Satan ---------------------------- 106
    k. The Judgment of the Dead -------------------- 117
5. Entering Eternity
    a. A New Heaven and a New Earth ------------ 124
    b. The Unveiling of New Jerusalem ---------- 141
    c. Inside the Cubed City, New Jerusalem -- 148
    d. The New Jerusalem, The Bride of the Lamb -- 153
6. What God Has Said is Truthful and He Loves You
    a. All of God's Words in Revelation are Trustworthy and True --------------------------- 173
7. Epilogue: Invitation and Warning ----------------- 181

    For More Study ------------------------------------- 187
    About the Author

Preface

This book focuses on what happens after Jesus' Return, after the Tribulation Period has ended. Chapters 20 – 22 in the book of Revelation addresses this time and forward. It is also spoken of and explained in the Old Testament and New Testament. I believe Hebrews 11: 8-10, 13-16, 39-40 puts one of the best synopsis to all of this. 8 By faith Abraham, when he was called, obeyed to go out to the place which he was to receive for an inheritance. He went out, not knowing where he went. 9 By faith he lived as an alien in the land of promise, as in a land not his own, dwelling in tents with Isaac and Jacob, the heirs with him of the same promise. 10 For he was looking for the city which has foundations, whose builder and maker is God. 13 These all died in faith, not having received the promises, but having seen them and embraced them from afar, and having confessed that they were strangers and pilgrims on the earth. 14 For those who say such things make it clear that they are seeking a country of their own. 15 If indeed they had been thinking of that country from which they went out, they would have had enough time to return. 16 But now they desire a better country, that is, a heavenly one. Therefore God is not ashamed of them, to be called their God, for he has prepared a city for them. 39 These all, having been commended for their faith, didn't receive the promise, 40 God having provided some better thing concerning us, so that apart from us they should not be made perfect. (WEB) *In verse 40 it notes that apart from us they should not be made perfect. I looked up in the Greek to see what verses 39 and 40 are alluding to in this. They, all those listed in Hebrews chapter eleven and so many more not overtly listed, did not receive the promises in their present lifetime as God foresaw much better fulfillments later. Once everything has unfolded, having reached the end stage in full strength we shall all together, without one person missing, receive all that has been promised to the countless generations over the millenniums. The Godhead is very excited anticipating the time He will finally be living right in the midst of us on earth and in New Jerusalem. His presence will be right here with us. Yes, He is presently living in each one of us who have accepted Jesus, Yeshua HaMashiach, as our Lord and Savior. His Spirit lives in us. However, He will be physically present with us, face to face. We will be able to intimately walk and talk with Him as it was meant to be back in Genesis before the fall of mankind. In light of Elohim being the grand architect that He is, He spends five chapters of His Word, Ezekiel 40 - 44, explaining the architecture of the place where He will be living with us during the Millennial Kingdom. This will be in fulfillment of all of the promises given to Israel. After the Millennium, our eternal home of New Jerusalem with our Lord, Immanuel, will be unveiled. What is incredible is that He has been working on what He promised us in John 14: 1-4 for thousands of years. What I found in my study of New Jerusalem is unbelievable. I can't wait to walk around in it with Yeshua and all of you. Maranatha!*

If you have not read the two previous books in this series, "What Paths Led Us Here?" and "What is Next Down These Tracks?" I would highly recommend them. The first book explains who God is, history lessons from the beginning of time to the End Times in relation to nations, Israel, and the Biblical Church. It also explains the reason for many of the troubles in the world. The second book goes from shortly before the Seals in Revelation to a few months after the Return of

Christ Jesus. As many of you have experienced, I, too, over several decades have learned varied thoughts and theories on what will happen after the Tribulation Period. I am so thankful for these teachings, especially from so many expert teachers of the Bible. I desired to research for myself directly from God's Word to find out exactly what He is saying. There is so much that He has spoken to us about this.

While working on this book, I have had the honor of reading many commentators from centuries ago to recent ones. I also read some of the biblical texts in the Greek and Hebrew original language with English notations and remarks given by translators. Additionally, I read a few of the texts in Aramaic, especially found in the book of Daniel. This language was periodically used in scripture once the Babylonian exile began, including some areas in the New Testament. Therefore, throughout this book, each time you see words in italics these are either my own notations or information taken from commentators, who are directly named when they are used. All of the words within parenthesis, (written here) *are God's name in Hebrew or important word meanings from the Hebrew, Aramaic, or Greek, which are taken from The Bible Hub resource. Bible Hub: Search, Read, Study the Bible in Many Languages. (2019). Biblehub.com.* https://biblehub.com/. *BibleHub is an excellent resource that I would strongly recommend to anyone who wishes to do an in-depth study of the Bible. I am thankful for the availability of the multitude of resources I have used over the innumerable months, too many to name. When I quote from any resources, they are referenced in the text. Then, all of the other words in regular font are the scriptures quoted from the World English Bible (WEB), or The New Heart English Bible (NHEB). The reason the versions of NHEB and*

WEB are used is that they are Public Domain versions. I am incredibly thankful for these versions as an enormous amount of scripture is used in this book. Without the availability of these two Public Domain versions in the present-day English language, all of the scripture mentioned in this book would have not been able to be included. Thank you, Wayne Mitchell, and Michael Paul Johnson for making these versions available in the Public Domain.

I understand that there are people who will not agree with what I have found in my study. I respect your thought process as this has been a subject debated through the centuries with not everyone agreeing. Thus, I am not dogmatic in proclaiming what I have written here is the absolute truth as only God and His Word is the absolute truth. I understand some of the people who read this will prefer other versions of the Bible. Please feel free to open up your Bible and to read all of the quoted scriptures directly from the Bible translation that you prefer. Also, some things for the upcoming future events we will only fully understand after we look back on it; similar to the people who lived during the time when Jesus walked the earth. Not everyone understood God's plan in that season of time clearly as they were expecting God to come as the reigning king, overthrowing the power of the Roman Empire and ushering in the Kingdom of God. They, including Jesus' disciples, were not expecting the Lamb of God, sacrificing Himself for the sins of mankind to bring all who would accept Him back into relationship with God. As they looked back on scripture after Jesus' resurrection and the indwelling Holy Spirit of God revealed it to them, they saw that it was clearly laid out from Genesis onward. Some people call it the Scarlet Thread in the Bible. I only ask that if you decide to read this book, to judge it against what God's Word says throughout its totality, like a thread that ties it all together. Be as the Bereans were in Acts 17:11-12: 11 Now these were more noble than those in Thessalonica, in that they received the word with all readiness of the mind, examining the Scriptures daily to see whether these things were so. 12 Many of them therefore believed; also of the prominent Greek women, and not a few men. (WEB) *I would like this to be a resource for you to read and make up your own mind as you begin your own study of God's Word. I desire many blessings of God upon you as you begin your quest to understand this subject as well.*

All of the Promises Given to Israel Fulfilled

Millennial Kingdom

At the commencement of the Millennial period, Satan will be bound for the entire period of time. An angel of God will bind him in large prison chains and throw him into the Abyss, which is the home of the dead and evil spirits. The Abyss will be locked and sealed shut. Therefore, he will not be doing his deceptive, accusatory work during this time period. It says this in Revelation 20: 1-3 ₁ I saw an angel coming down out of heaven, having the key of the abyss and a great chain in his hand. ₂ He seized the serpent, the ancient snake, which is the devil and Satan, and bound him for a thousand years, ₃ and cast him into the abyss, and shut it, and sealed it over him, that he should deceive the nations no more, until the thousand years were finished. After this, he must be freed for a short time. (NHEB)

Next, it seems that Jesus, alongside us, will execute judgment on all of the nations and people groups. We will also rule alongside Yeshua HaMashiach during the Millennium. This is addressed in Revelation 2: 26-27. ₂₆ He who overcomes, and he who keeps my works to the end, to him I will give authority over the nations. ₂₇ He will rule them with a rod of iron, shattering them like clay pots, as I also have received of my Father; (WEB) *This is also spoken of in Revelation 3: 21.* ₂₁ He who overcomes, I will give to him to sit down with me on my throne, as I also overcame and sat down with my Father on his throne. (WEB) *In Daniel 7: 27 it explains that the kingdoms under heaven will be handed over to the holy people to be ruled by them.* ₂₇ The kingdom and the dominion, and the greatness of the kingdoms under the whole sky, will be given to the people of the saints of the Most High. His kingdom is an everlasting kingdom, and all dominions will serve and obey him.' *(NHEB)* *Through the rulership under Yahweh we will possess the whole earth, which will be filled with the knowledge of Yahweh and His glory. People will call on His name. They will serve Him. This is stated in Habakkuk 2:14 and Zephaniah 3:9.* 14 For the earth will be filled with the knowledge of Yahweh's glory, as the waters cover the sea. 9 For then I will purify the lips of the peoples, that they may all call on Yahweh's name, to serve him shoulder to shoulder. (NHEB) *Each of us will be a partner to the Messiah in His divine administration. This is also alluded to in Luke 19: 11-27 Matthew 24: 45-47 and I Corinthians 6: 2. I also believe there is a connection shown here between Psalm 2: 7-12, in particular verse nine and Daniel 2: 33-35. Jesus will delegate to each one of us authority over a designated number of nations and/or people groups to execute judgment in the end. How many that will be I believe is dependent upon our life here on earth after salvation. This is a whole other study. I encourage you to look into this as you are led.*

All of the Believers in God throughout history, who served Him, will come to life for the thousand years as First Corinthians fifteen says. I Corinthians 15: 20-28 20 But now Christ has been raised from the dead. He became the first fruits of those who are asleep. 21 For since death came by man, the resurrection of the dead also came by man. 22 For as in Adam all die, so also in Christ all will be made alive. 23 But each in his own order: Christ the firstfruits, then those who are Christ's, at his coming. 24 Then the end comes, when he will deliver up the Kingdom to God, even the Father; when he will have abolished all rule and all authority and power. 25 For he must reign until he has put all his enemies under his feet. 26 The last enemy that will be abolished is death. 27 For, "He put all things in subjection under his feet." But when he says, "All things are put in subjection," it is evident that he is excepted who subjected all things to him. 28 When all things have been subjected to him, then the Son will also himself be subjected to him who subjected all things to him, that God may be all in all. (WEB) *We will be able to continue fulfilling our life goals and promises made to us by God. This is the first resurrection. The saints of God under the authority of Jesus will exercise dominion over the earth in whichever area of the earth we are individually or as a team sent. We will be rulers over the nations that survived through to the end of the Tribulation period and enter into the Millennium alive. Of course, we will not be doing this alone. We will have direct access to God to ensure that we are making the best decision. I am so thankful for this understanding. Thank you, Lord Jesus! It says this in* Isaiah 2:3-5. 3 And many peoples shall come and say, "Come, let's go up to the mountain of the LORD (Yahweh), and to the house of the God (Elohim) of Jacob; and he will teach us of his ways, and we will walk in his paths." For out of Zion the law shall go forth, and the word of the LORD (Yahweh) from Jerusalem. 4 He will judge between the nations, and will decide (*rebuke, render decisions*) concerning many peoples; and they shall beat their swords into plowshares, and their spears into pruning hooks. Nation shall not lift up sword against nation, neither shall they learn war any more. 5 House of Jacob, come, and let us walk in the light of

the LORD (Yahweh). (NHEB) *We will judge in the same way God judges, meaning not by outward appearance, rather by righteousness as it says in* Isaiah 11: 3-5. 3 His delight will be in the fear of Yahweh. He will not judge by the sight of his eyes, neither decide by the hearing of his ears;
4 but with righteousness he will judge the poor, and decide with equity for the humble of the earth. He will strike the earth with the rod of his mouth; and with the breath of his lips he will kill the wicked. 5 Righteousness will be the belt of his waist, and faithfulness the belt of his waist. (WEB) *As previously stated in Revelation 20: 4-6 that those of us who have died in Christ Jesus and have been resurrected will be given thrones so that we will have the power to judge righteously. Those of us who were beheaded for Jesus and the word of God will exercise under divinely granted kingly power with Christ Jesus. All of us who are resurrected during this first resurrection are truly blessed as we are set apart in possessing eternal life with Yahweh. The second death will have no authority over us. For the thousand years we will be busy with a sacred lifestyle offering sacrifices unto God and exercising dominion with Christ Jesus.* Revelation 20: 4-6 4 I saw thrones, and they sat on them, and judgment (*authority to judge*) was given to them. I saw the souls of those who had been beheaded for the testimony of Jesus, and for the word of God, and such as did not worship the beast nor his image, and did not receive the mark on their forehead and on their hand. They lived, and reigned with Christ for a thousand years. 5 The rest of the dead did not live until the thousand years were finished. This is the first resurrection. 6 Blessed and holy is he who has part in

the first resurrection. Over these, the second death has no power, but they will be priests of God and of Christ, and will reign with him one thousand years. (NHEB) *It is also spoken of in* Revelation 2: 26-27. 26 He who overcomes, and he who keeps my works (*doing the actions and deeds that God has asked one to do*) to the end, to him I will give authority over the nations. 27 He will rule them with a rod of iron, shattering them like clay pots; as I also have received of my Father. (WEB)

    God will bring His creation back to the way He made it in the Garden of Eden. Animals will no longer be eating each other. They will return to eating vegetation only. This is described in Isaiah 11:6-9. 6 The wolf will live with the lamb, and the leopard will lie down with the young goat; The calf and the young lion will graze together; and a little child will lead them. 7 The cow and the bear will graze. [*Interesting sidenote, while I lived in Alaska, I saw grizzly bears grazing in Denali National Park in the summer. So yes, though bears are presently omnivores, they can be vegetarians during certain periods of time in this present age.*] Their young ones will lie down together. The lion will eat straw like the ox. 8 The nursing child will play near a cobra's hole, and the weaned child will put his hand on the viper's den. 9 They will not hurt nor destroy in all my holy mountain; for the earth will be full of the knowledge of the LORD, as the waters cover the sea. (NHEB)

People will no longer die young, but will be able to see the works of their hands fulfilled. Isaiah 65: 20-25:
₂₀ "There shall be no more there an infant of days, nor an old man who has not filled his days; for the child shall die one hundred years old, and the sinner being one hundred years old shall be accursed.
₂₁ They shall build houses, and inhabit them; and they shall plant vineyards, and eat the fruit of them.
₂₂ They shall not build, and another inhabit; they shall not plant, and another eat: for as the days of a tree shall be the days of my people, and my chosen shall long enjoy the work of their hands.
₂₃ They shall not labor in vain, nor bring forth for calamity; for they are the seed of the blessed of Yahweh, and their offspring with them.
₂₄ It shall happen that, before they call, I will answer; and while they are yet speaking, I will hear. ₂₅ The wolf and the lamb shall feed together, and the lion shall eat straw like the ox; and dust shall be the serpent's food. They shall not hurt nor destroy in all my holy mountain," says Yahweh. (WEB)

As previously mentioned, the Millennial Kingdom is when God fulfills all of His promises to Abraham, Isaac, Jacob, and all of His words written to Israel. He is a God of His word. What He promises, He shall fulfill, without question, as it says in II Corinthians 1: 20-22.
₂₀ For however many are the promises of God, in him is the "Yes." Therefore also through him is the "Amen," to the glory of God through us. ₂₁ Now he who establishes us with you in Christ, and anointed us, is God; ₂₂ who also sealed us (*attesting we are His, in today's terms - all the legal documents have been signed and recorded to authenticate ownership*), and

gave us the down payment (*present part payment guaranteeing the full payment is without question coming*) of the Spirit in our hearts. (WEB) *Additionally, there are so many promises written in scripture for the Church of God as there are also for the nation of Israel that they could easily fill a large book explaining them all.*

Some of God's promises to Christians is that we will be truly with Him in unbroken fellowship with Elohim. Everything He has is shared with us and everything we have is shared with Him. This is promised in II Peter 1:3-4. 3 seeing that his divine power has granted to us all things that pertain to life and godliness, through the knowledge of him who called us by his own glory and virtue, 4 by which he has granted to us his precious and exceedingly great promises; that through these you may become partakers of the divine nature, having escaped from the corruption that is in the world by lust. (WEB) *We will also have unbroken fellowship with God as Adam and Eve had in the Garden of Eden before the fall. We will not have to strive to be 'godly,' without any sin, as the righteousness of Christ Jesus fully clothes us. We can rest in this. All that had been sinful in our lives will have been permanently removed from us. This is alluded to in Hebrews 4:9-10.* 9 There remains therefore a Sabbath rest for the people of God. 10 For he who has entered into his rest has himself also rested from his works, as God did from his. (WEB)

Now I will be focusing God's explicit promises to Israel during this thousand-year period. In this section, I will discuss Israel living in their land, the nations of the world honoring the Lord God and Israel as well as God living in their midst in the restored Temple of God. There are four reasons why I will be focusing on this. The main reason is that it is the whole heart of God desiring to be with us. It is out of His love that we have been created, as well as all of the angels and the entirety of creation. His heart's desire is to have fellowship and communion with us. His love for us is so great that He even sent His own Son, Jesus, to die for us so relationship might be re-established with Him for any who desire to accept His invitation. Also, God has literally spent chapters of the Bible explaining the coming Temple where He will be interacting with His people. Therefore, since God is so focused on this, I thought it would be good to look at the Temple as well. Remember, we, as the Body of Christ, are Jesus' bride. Presently, individually, each Believer in Christ Jesus is a bodily Temple of God. We are mobile houses of His indwelling Spirit. In the Millennium and thereafter, we will be right there physically with Him. Of course, during the Millennium rule we will not be receiving the praise and worship of the people, that is for God alone. A third reason is due to humans' propensity to walk away from God trying to control life on their own terms. This is made evident throughout the scripture. After the Fall recorded in Genesis people began living life on their own terms, seeking to be in charge of what happens to them. Adam, who knew and walked with God was still alive when Noah's father, Lamech, was alive. They could talk directly with Adam to learn what life before sin entered the world was like. Just before the flood every thought a person had that poured out into their actions was pure evil, as far away from the character of God as possible. Additionally, after the flood in Genesis chapters six to eleven evidence how humans as a whole are so twisted by sin that even after all of the experiences of the flood and the effects of it still walk away from God and His ways. They try to govern life on their own through creating their own idols to bring a sense of control over others and oneself. Abram, before being called by God was from a household who worshipped idols as referenced in Joshua 24:23. Abraham could have known Shem, Noah's son, if they still spoke the same language. Even Isaac could have met him when he was young. What they could have talked about, recollecting what happened before the flood and after it. In the book of Exodus, it shows how Israel, even after being miraculously delivered from Egypt took to being upset and not turning to God. One may read Exodus 15: 22-26, chapters 16, 17: 1-7 and chapter 32 to see this in action. Humans continue to walk away from God even to this present time. Thus, during the Millennial time period, God literally lives right with people on earth, specifically in the land of Israel. As will be seen, at the end of the Millennial, an enormous throng of people turn against God. The last reason why I am focusing on the promises given to Israel during the Millennium is that they are explicitly explained in scripture. The role of us, the Body of Christ, saved by His grace is more of a mystery, alluded to in scripture, both Old and New Testament verses, but not often explicitly explained.

The initial promise to Abraham was God calling him to leave his country to the land that He had promised to him and that God would make him into a great nation. The following verses are examples of this promise.

Genesis 12: 1-9

1 Now the LORD (Yahweh) had said to Abram, "Go out from your country, and from your relatives, and from your father's house, to the land that I will show you. 2 And I will make of you a great nation. And I will bless you and make your name great. And you will be a blessing. 3 And I will bless those who bless you, and I will curse those who treat you with contempt, and through you all the families of the earth will be blessed."

4 So Abram left, as the LORD (Yahweh) had told him, and Lot went with him. Abram was seventy-five years old when he departed from Haran. 5 Abram took Sarai his wife, Lot his brother's son, and all their possessions that they had accumulated, and the people whom they had acquired in Haran, and they left to go to the land of Canaan. And they came to the land of Canaan, 6 and Abram passed through the land to the place of Shechem, to the oak of Moreh. At that time the Canaanites were in the land. 7 The LORD (Yahweh) appeared to Abram and said to him, "I will give this land to your offspring." He built an altar there to the LORD (Yahweh), who appeared to him. 8 He left from there to the mountain on the east of Bethel, and pitched his tent, having Bethel on the west, and Ai on the east. There he built an altar to the LORD (Yahweh) and called on the name of the LORD (Yahweh). 9 And Abram traveled on, continuing toward the Negev.
(NHEB)

Genesis 13: 14-18

14 Yahweh said to Abram, after Lot was separated from him, "Now, lift up your eyes, and look from the place where you are, northward and southward and eastward and westward, 15 for all the land which you

see, I will give to you, and to your offspring forever. ₁₆ I will make your offspring as the dust of the earth, so that if a man can number the dust of the earth, then your seed (*offspring*) may also be numbered. ₁₇ Arise, walk through the land in its length and in its breadth; for I will give it to you." ₁₈ Abram moved his tent, and came and lived by the oaks of Mamre, which are in Hebron, and built an altar there to Yahweh. (WEB)

Genesis 15: 17-20
₁₇ It came to pass that, when the sun went down, and it was dark, look, a smoking fire pot and a flaming torch passed between these pieces.
₁₈ On that day the LORD (Yahweh) made a covenant with Abram, saying, "To your descendants I have given this land, from the river of Egypt to the great river, the river Perath (*Euphrates, Perath being its older name*): ₁₉ the Kenites, the Kenizzites, the Kadmonites, ₂₀ the Hethites, the Perizzites, the Rephaim, ₂₁ the Amorites, the Canaanites, the Hivites, the Girgashites, and the Jebusites." (NHEB)

Daniel 12: 13
₁₃ But go you (Daniel) your way until the end; for you shall rest (extended rest from labor), and shall stand in your lot (allotted inheritance), at the end of the days. (WEB)

Jerusalem, City of God

Yahweh will send messengers, His angels, out to those who have survived throughout the nations of the world to proclaim the glory of the Lord as well as to bring them to Jerusalem. Miserable, deep darkness will cover the earth, but Yahweh's light will rise upon them. His glory will appear over them. Messengers of God will go out and bring in people from such nations as Midian and Ephah. Midian was a descendant of Abraham by Keturah, his wife after Sarah died, who lived east and south of the Dead Sea as well as the coastal strip of the Sinai Peninsula and parts of the Arabian Peninsula. They are spoken of in Genesis 25: 6, 37:28, Exodus 2:16-25, Numbers 10:29, and chapter 31, as well as Judges chapters 6-7. Ephah was the oldest son of Midian, who lived along the shore of the Dead Sea. He was spoken of in Genesis 25:4. They will come from Tarshish, who are descendants of Javan, the fourth son of Japheth. The area of Tarsus encompasses Anatolia and Ionians, one of the first Greek nations along the shores and islands of Asia Minor, present day south-central Turkey as well as Crete, Aegean, Tyrrhenian Seas, and parts of Asia Minor. However, all these islands will be gone at this time. They will come from Libya, which includes Pul, near Egypt and Ethiopia. More people will come from Lydia, who are descendants of Lud, the fourth son of Shem. This area is associated with Lydia, which is in Asia Minor, present day western Turkey. They were one of the first nations to make gold coins. They were also renowned archers. There will also be people coming from Tubal, who was the fifth son of Japheth. His descendants originated southeast of the Black Sea, where Turkey currently is located. His descendants were the Iberians, who moved to the Iberian Peninsula of Spain, Portugal, and Andorra as well as to Siberia in Russia. Additionally, there will be people coming from Greece. An interesting side note as there were both the Hellenistic Jews and the Jewish people mentioned in Acts chapter six. The Hellenistic Jews were people born Jewish or were proselytes to Judaism who spoke Greek and not Hebrew or Aramaean. There will also be people coming from more distant regions. The verses of Isaiah 60:8-9 are quite intriguing. 8 "Who are these who fly as a cloud, and as the doves to their windows (*nests/roosts*)? 9 Surely the islands (*coastlands*) shall wait for me, and the ships of Tarshish first, to bring your sons from far, their silver and their gold with them, for the name of the LORD (Yahweh) your God (Elohim), and for the Holy One of Israel, because he has glorified you. (NHEB) *Just an interesting observation, will there still be air flights and sea travel continuing to happen at this time? They will bring to Israel offerings, bearing gifts and proclaiming the praise of Yahweh. Sheba will bring gold and frankincense. Sheba is possibly from south of Egypt in the area of Ethiopia, spoken of in Psalm 72:15 and Jeremiah 6:20. Sheba might also be a possible descendant of Abraham through Keturah, mentioned in Genesis 25:3. Kedar will bring flocks of sheep and rams of Nebaioth to be used as offerings to Yahweh Elohim, the Holy One of Israel. Kedar is a descendent of Ishmael, nomads in the Arabian Desert area, spoken of in Genesis 25:13. Nebaioth was the oldest son of Ishmael. His descendants lived around Petra and the surrounding region. They are spoken of in Genesis 25:13 and I Chronicles 1:29.*

Jerusalem, the City of Yahweh, will be exalted and honored. Yahweh will give Jerusalem a new name as well as a royal turban from the open palm of His hand. As Isaiah 62:4b says, 4 *...you (Zion) shall be called Hephzibah (My delight is in you), and your land Beulah (Married); for Yahweh delights in you, and your land shall be married.* (WEB) *God will rejoice over Jerusalem. It shall be fully known that Yahweh is your Deliverer and Gaal, Kinsman Redeemer. Those who live in the city will also be called the Holy People, the Redeemed of the Lord. He will also call them the Sought Out as they were sought out with great care and cherished deeply. They will be called a kingdom of priests, as it is explained in I Peter 2:9 and Revelation 1:6. We will be robed in priestly attire as we minister unto Elohim, clothed in His righteousness. In reward for our service unto God, we will be fed and provided for through the wealth of the nations. Jerusalem is a City Not Forsaken. In fact, the sun will no longer be what lights up the day or the moon that lights up the night. The glorious splendor of Elohim will light up Jerusalem. Jerusalem's walls will be called Salvation and its gates are called Praise. Isaiah 62:1 speaks to this.* 1 *For Zion's sake I will not keep silent (inactive, unresponsive), and for Jerusalem's sake I will not rest, until her righteousness go forth as brightness, and her salvation (יְשׁוּעָה Yeshuah) as a lamp that burns.* (NHEB)

My mind was blown here as I read Isaiah 62:1. The word 'salvation' is how Jesus' name is pronounced in Messianic circles. This is the Hebrew name for Jesus. The Hebrew writing noted here is the contemporary version, not used in ancient scripture. The ancient Hebrew did not have vowel notations and the shapes were a little different. Joshua is יְהוֹשֻׁעַ Yehoshua (The Lord is my salvation) is very close to this name. In the Hebrew Bible, Jesus' name is יֵשׁוּעַ and is also pronounced Ye-SHEW-ə. The very last sound, which is not included here, is found in neither English nor Greek. It includes a rough, guttural sound, almost like what is found in the German and Arab languages. Thus, the majority of people do not include this last sound. During the time of Zerubabel, when the second Temple was being built, the name Yehoshua was shortened to Yeshua. In the time period when Jesus lived on earth, many of the Jewish people spoke Aramaic. Therefore, he might have been called 'Isho' - ee-SHŌ during his lifetime. Jesus as English people say it is His name pronounced in the Latin language. However, we say His name, it is all to His glory and reverence.

Yahweh will ensure that we will have true righteousness through enjoying our salvation, having been delivered and redeemed. The nations will see the righteousness of Jerusalem and will rebuild her walls. The gates of Jerusalem will continually remain open, never shut day or night. The wealth of the nations will be brought in with their kings leading the way in triumph. For instance, Lebanon will bring what they are famous for, their aromatic hardwood for building materials. They will bring it into Jerusalem for God's sanctuary. As Isaiah 60:17 describes that instead of bronze, God will bring in gold. Instead of iron, God will bring in silver. Instead of wood, God will bring in bronze. Instead of stones, God will bring in iron. The nations will satisfy every need that Jerusalem has. The descendants of the people who used to torment Israel will come and bow before your feet and call Jerusalem the City of the Holy One, Qadosh, of Israel. The nations will also renew the ancient cities of Israel that were deserted for generations. Foreigners will shepherd the flocks of sheep and their descendants will work the fields and vineyards in Israel. It will be a joy for all involved for generations to come. Yahweh will reward the people for their faithful work unto Him. From His presence will go forth His reward to each person who brings forth work to Him that is done to the best of their own ability.

A highway will be built for the nations to come to Jerusalem. It will descend from the gates of the city. All obstacles will be removed and any unevenness from the natural, rocky soil will be removed. The highway will be called the Road of Holiness. It will only be open to those who live in the manner of holiness to God. Any impure person who despises wisdom, is quarrelsome or mocks when found to be guilty will not be allowed to place a foot onto it. Along this highway there will not be any violent beast found. Only those redeemed by the Kinsman-Redeemer, Yeshua HaMashiach will be allowed to walk on it. These people will enter Jerusalem singing praises unto Yahweh as everlasting gladness and rejoicing will crown their heads.

People from the nations that are left will come up to Jerusalem, up to God's Temple to learn of His ways, incorporating His wisdom, commands, and characteristics into their way of life. He will willingly give them instruction in the ways of righteousness. Elohim will decide controversies between mighty nations, even those located in remote locations as well as disputes between many groups of people, making judicial decisions. The people who have been exiled, dispersed throughout the nations will be gathered back together. The nations that were dwindling, having no power of their own, will grow into a nation mighty in number. Then the LORD will rule over them in Mount Zion from that day and forever. In response to these problems being solved they will no longer go to war or harm one another. They will focus on doing the work that they enjoy as well as working the land to support one another. Each person will securely dwell in their own home area, with no one to trouble them. Instead of shame, God will give each person a double portion assigned to each one as their inheritance. All this will be judiciously handed out during the previously mentioned judgment time of God. Everlasting joy of heart will be theirs. Yahweh will proclaim the year of His favor upon them, comforting them by making sure true justice is given. Instead of feeling worthless, He will give them a crown of beauty, pouring over them the oil of joy and giving them a garment of praise showing how favored they are in His sight. He will adorn each person with jewels. Do you remember the parable of the lady with the ten silver coins, drachmas, in Luke 15:8-10? Each drachma had the value of one day's worth of wages. The bride was lavishly dressed from head to toe with the best jewels and adornment that her family could afford. Another example of this is found in Psalm 45:13-14. He will call them Terebinth of righteousness, enjoying the surety that Yahweh is a covenant-keeping God. A Terebinth is an aromatic, multipurpose resin tree of the cashew family. It is a prominent, lofty tree, growing up to 33 feet tall, having a very strong root system that allows it to withstand the toughest of times.

As stated earlier, God will raise up the mountain upon which Jerusalem sits and the other mountains and hills around it will sink. In addition, near the end of the tribulation period, just before He returns, the mountains of the earth will sink down. It appears from what is written in His Word that the mountain where Jerusalem is located will be the highest of all of the mountains of the world. The Himalayan area, which incorporates many of the highest mountains of the world, will have a long way to sink as well as a number of the other mountains of the world, such as Mt. Aconcagua in Argentina, Mt. Denali (McKinley) in Alaska, Mt. Kilimanjaro in Africa, Mt. Elbrus in Russia, Mt. Vinson Massif in Antarctica, and Mt. Puncak Jaya in New Guinea. I believe even though New Guinea is the second largest island in the world, behind Greenland, it may or may not disappear altogether as the Lord's Word says the islands of the world will disappear. However, there are many different kinds of islands. Some islands are part of a continental shelf, such as New Guinea, being part of the Australian continent. Some are barrier islands created from sand or moraines left over from glacial melting, such as Long Island. Other islands are oceanic islands created by volcanic action erupting from the ocean floor, such as Hawaii as well as Japan from sitting atop four tectonic plates. There are also islands made from the coral reefs, such as the Caribbean islands. Some of the islands are manmade, created by reeds and earth as well as some using recycled materials. Just an interesting fact, Australia is not considered to be an island, rather a continent, because it is the largest landmass on its continental shelf. Greenland is part of the American Continental Shelf, smaller than the

American landmass, thus it is called an island. Some people debate New Zealand being on its own continental shelf, Zealandia, with 94% of its landmass being below water. I guess we shall see what happens when the time comes as some of these islands are on continental shelves and may not disappear. Will the continents return to their original locations, being back together again rather than being separated by oceans? Something to look forward to finding out when it happens. It also says in Isaiah 61:4 that the torn down places will be rebuilt. Yes, it references Jerusalem specifically; however, I believe it is a promise to all areas also destroyed by the sin of previous generations throughout the earth. Therefore, during the Millennium, as the people return to their homelands and spread out, what was destroyed will be rebuilt. I am sure it will not be rebuilt as it was previously, like a carbon copy, but as they see fit for their needs. The following are many scriptures addressing what has been written above.

Isaiah 2: 2-4
2 It shall happen in the latter days, that the mountain of the LORD's (Yahweh's) house shall be established on the top of the mountains, and shall be raised above the hills; and all nations shall flow to it.
3 And many peoples shall come and say, "Come, let's go up to the mountain of the LORD (Yahweh), and to the house of the God (Elohim) of Jacob; and he will teach us of his ways, and we will walk in his paths." For out of Zion the law shall go forth, and the word of the LORD (Yahweh) from Jerusalem.
4 He will judge between the nations, and will decide concerning many peoples; and they shall beat their swords into plowshares, and their spears into pruning

hooks. Nation shall not lift up sword against nation, neither shall they learn war any more. (NHEB)

Micah 4: 1- 8
₁ But in the latter days, it will happen that the mountain of Yahweh's temple will be established on the top of the mountains, and it will be exalted above the hills; and peoples will stream to it.
₂ Many nations will go and say, "Come, and let us go up to the mountain of Yahweh, and to the house of the God (Elohim) of Jacob; and he will teach us of his ways, and we will walk in his paths." For out of Zion will go forth the law, and the word of Yahweh from Jerusalem;
₃ and he will judge between many peoples, and will decide concerning strong nations afar off. They will beat their swords into plowshares, and their spears into pruning hooks. Nation will not lift up sword against nation, neither will they learn war any more.
₄ But they will sit every man under his vine and under his fig tree; and no one will make them afraid: For the mouth of Yahweh of Armies (Tsaba) has spoken.
₅ Indeed all the nations may walk in the name of their gods; but we will walk in the name of Yahweh our God forever and ever.
₆ "In that day," says Yahweh, "I will assemble that which is lame, and I will gather that which is driven away, and that which I have afflicted;
₇ and I will make that which was lame a remnant, and that which was cast far off a strong nation: and Yahweh will reign over them on Mount Zion from then on, even forever."
₈ You, tower (*watchtower*) of the flock, the hill of the daughter of Zion, to you it will come, yes, the former

dominion will come, the kingdom of the daughter of Jerusalem. (WEB)

Isaiah 66: 18-21
18 "For I know their works and their thoughts. I am coming to gather all nations and languages; and they will come and see my glory. 19 "I will set a sign among them, and I will send such as escape (*fugitives*) of them to the nations, to Tarshish, Pul, and Lud, who draw the bow, to Tubal and Javan, to the islands afar off, who have not heard my fame, neither have seen my glory; and they shall declare my glory among the nations. 20 They shall bring all your brothers out of all the nations for an offering to the LORD (Yahweh), on horses, and in chariots, and in litters, and on mules, and on dromedaries, to my holy mountain Jerusalem, says the LORD (Yahweh), as the children of Israel bring their offering in a clean vessel into the house of the LORD (Yahweh). 21 And I will also take some of them for myself as priests and Levites," says the LORD (Yahweh). (NHEB)

Isaiah 60: 1-22
1 "Arise, shine; for your light is come, and the glory of Yahweh is risen on you. 2 For, behold, darkness shall cover the earth, and gross darkness the peoples; but Yahweh will arise on you, and his glory shall be seen on you.
3 Nations shall come to your light, and kings to the brightness of your rising.
4 "Lift up your eyes all around, and see: they all gather themselves together, they come to you; your sons shall come from far, and your daughters shall be carried in the arms.

₅ Then you shall see and be radiant, and your heart shall thrill and be enlarged; because the abundance of the sea shall be turned to you, the wealth of the nations shall come to you.
₆ The multitude of camels shall cover you, the dromedaries of Midian and Ephah; all they from Sheba shall come; they shall bring gold and frankincense, and shall proclaim the praises of Yahweh.
₇ All the flocks of Kedar shall be gathered together to you, the rams of Nebaioth shall minister to you; they shall come up with acceptance on my altar; and I will glorify the house of my glory.
₈ "Who are these who fly as a cloud, and as the doves to their windows (*nests/roosts*)?
₉ Surely the islands (*maritime countries, coastlands*) shall wait for me, and the ships of Tarshish first, to bring your sons from far, their silver and their gold with them, for the name of Yahweh your God (Elohim), and for the Holy One (Qadosh) of Israel, because he has glorified you.
₁₀ "Foreigners shall build up your walls, and their kings shall minister to you: for in my wrath I struck you, but in my favor have I had mercy on you.
₁₁ Your gates also shall be open continually; they shall not be shut day nor night; that men may bring to you the wealth of the nations, and their kings led captive (*led in triumphal procession*).
₁₂ For that nation and kingdom that will not serve you shall perish; yes, those nations shall be utterly wasted.
₁₃ "The glory of Lebanon shall come to you, the fir tree, the pine, and the box (*cypress*) tree together, to beautify the place of my sanctuary; and I will make the

place of my feet glorious.

₁₄ The sons of those who afflicted (*oppressed*) you shall come bending to you; and all those who despised you shall bow themselves down at the soles of your feet; and they shall call you The city of Yahweh, The Zion of the Holy One of Israel.

₁₅ "Whereas you have been forsaken and hated, so that no man passed through you, I will make you an eternal excellency, a joy of many generations.

₁₆ You shall also drink the milk of the nations, and shall nurse from royal breasts; and you shall know that I, Yahweh, am your Savior (*Yasha, Deliverer*), and your Redeemer (*Gaal, Kinsman Redeemer*), the Mighty One (*Abir*) of Jacob.

₁₇ For brass I will bring gold, and for iron I will bring silver, and for wood brass, and for stones iron. I will also make your officers peace, and righteousness your ruler.

₁₈ Violence shall no more be heard in your land, desolation nor destruction within your borders; but you shall call your walls Salvation, and your gates Praise.

₁₉ The sun shall be no more your light by day; neither for brightness shall the moon give light to you: but Yahweh will be to you an everlasting light, and your God (Elohim) your glory.

₂₀ Your sun shall no more go down, neither shall your moon withdraw itself; for Yahweh will be your everlasting light, and the days of your mourning shall be ended.

₂₁ Your people also shall be all righteous; they shall inherit the land forever, the branch of my planting, the work of my hands, that I may be glorified.

₂₂ The little one shall become a thousand, and the

small one a strong nation; I, Yahweh, will hasten it in its time." (WEB)

Isaiah 62: 1-12

1 For Zion's sake I will not keep silent, and for Jerusalem's sake I will not rest, until her righteousness go forth as brightness, and her salvation as a lamp that burns.

2 The nations shall see your righteousness, and all kings your glory, and you shall be called by a new name, which the mouth of the LORD (*Yhvh, Yahweh, Jehovah, The Existing One, I am He who I am, Absolute and unchangeable one, Life-giver, Creator*) shall name.

3 You shall also be a crown of beauty in the hand of the LORD (Yahweh), and a royal diadem in the hand of your God.

4 And you shall no more be termed Forsaken; neither shall your land any more be termed Desolate: but you shall be called Hephzibah, and your land Beulah; for the LORD (Yahweh) delights in you, and your land shall be married.

5 For just as a young man marries a virgin, so your sons shall marry you; and as the bridegroom rejoices over the bride, so your God (Elohim) will rejoice over you.

6 I have set watchmen on your walls, Jerusalem; they shall never be silent, day or night. You who call on the LORD (Yahweh), take no rest,

7 and give him no rest until he establishes and until he makes Jerusalem a praise in the earth.

8 The LORD (Yahweh) has sworn by his right hand, and by the arm of his strength, "Surely I will no more give your grain to be food for your enemies; and foreigners shall not drink your new wine, for which you have

labored:

9 but those who have garnered (*harvested*) it shall eat it, and praise the LORD (Yahweh); and those who have gathered it shall drink it in the courts of my sanctuary."

10 Go through the gates, prepare the way of the people. Build up, build up the highway. Gather out the stones. Lift up a banner for the peoples.

11 Look, the LORD (Yahweh) has proclaimed to the remotest part of earth, "Say to the daughter of Zion, 'Look, your salvation comes. Look, his reward is with him, and his recompense before him.'"

12 They shall call them The holy (Qodesh) people, The redeemed (Gaal) of the LORD (Yahweh): and you shall be called Sought out, A city not forsaken. (NHEB)

Isaiah 61: 2-11

2 to proclaim the year of Yahweh's favor, and the day of vengeance of our God (Elohim); to comfort all who mourn;

3 to appoint to those who mourn in Zion, to give to them a garland for ashes, the oil of joy for mourning, the garment of praise for the spirit of heaviness; that they may be called trees of righteousness, the planting of Yahweh, that he may be glorified.

4 They shall build the old wastes (*ancient ruins*), they shall raise up the former desolations, and they shall repair the waste (*ruined*) cities, the desolations of many generations.

5 Strangers shall stand (*shepherd*) and feed your flocks, and foreigners shall be your plowmen and your vinedressers.

6 But you shall be named the priests of Yahweh; men will call you the ministers of our God (Elohim): you will

eat the wealth of the nations, and you will boast in their glory (*abundance, riches*).

7 Instead of your shame [you shall have] double; and instead of dishonor they shall rejoice in their portion (*inheritance*): therefore in their land they shall possess double; everlasting joy shall be to them.

8 "For I, Yahweh, love justice, I hate robbery with iniquity; and I will give them their recompense in truth, and I will make an everlasting covenant with them.

9 Their seed (*descendants*) shall be known among the nations, and their offspring among the peoples; all who see them shall acknowledge them, that they are the seed which Yahweh has blessed."

10 I will greatly rejoice in Yahweh, my soul shall be joyful in my God (*Elohim, True God, Trinity*); for he has clothed me with the garments of salvation, he has covered me with the robe of righteousness, as a bridegroom decks himself with a garland (*formal, elaborate turban*), and as a bride adorns herself with her jewels.

11 For as the earth brings forth its bud, and as the garden causes the things that are sown in it to spring forth; so the Lord (Adonai) Yahweh (*Yhvh, Jehovah, The Existing One, I am He who I am, Absolute and unchangeable one, Life-giver, Creator*) will cause righteousness and praise to spring forth before all the nations. (WEB)

Isaiah 35: 8-10

8 And a highway will be there, and it will be called the Way of Holiness. The unclean shall not pass over (*journey*) it, but it will be for those who walk in the Way. Wicked fools will not go there.

9 No lion will be there, nor will any ravenous animal go

up on it. They will not be found there; but the redeemed will walk there.

10 The LORD's (Yahweh's) ransomed ones will return, and come with singing to Zion; and everlasting joy will be on their heads. They will obtain gladness and joy, and sorrow and sighing will flee away." (NHEB)

Celebration of the Feast of Tabernacles

There will only be one required time for every single person on the earth to come to Jerusalem to worship the Lord God. All other times of the year they will be able to remain where they are and live out their lives. This one time will be the celebration of a feast that was instituted by God and written down by Moses thousands of years ago. Exodus 23: 16 16 And the feast of harvest (*Festival of the Harvest*), the first fruits of your labors, which you sow in the field: and the feast of harvest, at the end of the year, when you gather in your labors out of the field. (WEB) Leviticus 23: 33-43 33 The LORD (Yahweh) spoke to Moses, saying, 34 "Speak to the children of Israel, and say, 'On the fifteenth day of this seventh month is the feast of booths (*Feast of Tabernacles/Temporary Shelters, Pilgrimage Feast*) for seven days to the LORD (Yahweh). 35 On the first day shall be a holy convocation (*assembly*): you shall do no regular work (*one's normal occupation, business or service is not to be done*). 36 Seven days you shall offer an offering made by fire (*burnt offerings*) to the LORD (Yahweh). On the eighth day shall be a holy convocation (*assembly*) to you; and you shall offer an offering made by fire to the LORD (Yahweh). It is a solemn assembly; you shall do no regular work. 37 "'These are the appointed feasts of the LORD (Yahweh), which you shall proclaim to be holy convocations (*assembly*), to offer an offering (*burnt offerings*) made by fire to the LORD (Yahweh), a burnt offering, and a meal (*grain*) offering, a sacrifice, and drink offerings, each on its own day; 38 besides the Sabbaths of the LORD (Yahweh), and besides your gifts, and besides all your vows, and besides all your freewill (*voluntary, of your own decision*) offerings, which you give to the LORD (Yahweh). 39 "'So on the fifteenth day of the seventh month, when you have gathered in the fruits of the land, you shall keep (*make the pilgrimage to celebrate with feasting, dancing, and festivities*) the feast of the LORD (Yahweh) seven days: on the first day shall be a solemn rest, and on the eighth day shall be a solemn rest. 40 You shall take on the first day the fruit of goodly (*luxuriant, majestic, beautiful*) trees, branches of palm trees, and boughs of thick trees, and willows of the brook; and you shall rejoice before the LORD (Yahweh) your God (Elohim) seven days. 41 You shall keep it a feast to the LORD (Yahweh) seven days in the year: it is a statute forever throughout your generations; you shall keep it in the seventh month. 42 You shall dwell in booths (*temporary shelters*) seven days. All who are native-born in Israel shall dwell in booths, 43 that your generations may know (*clearly understand, comprehend, experience, be familiar with*) that I made the children of Israel to dwell in booths, when I brought them out of the land of Egypt. I am the LORD (Yahweh) your God (Elohim).'" (NHEB)

In the past, as the Israelis made their annual trek to Jerusalem to celebrate the Feast of Tabernacles, they would sing the Psalms as they ascended up the mountain. What a glorious, cherished memory it would be for everyone involved if they, too, also sing these same Psalms as they make their trip to Jerusalem. It is too much to include here. However, read Psalms 120 to 134 to see what the Songs of Ascent were. Jesus celebrated the Feast of Tabernacles during his lifetime on earth. In fact, one of his times of observing it as recorded in scripture is when he called out to everyone in John 7: 37-39. 37 Now on the last and greatest day of the feast, Jesus stood and cried out, "If anyone is thirsty, let him come to me and drink! 38 He who believes in me, as the Scripture has said, from within him will flow rivers of living water." 39 But he said this about the Spirit, which those believing in him were to receive. For the Holy Spirit was not yet given, because Jesus wasn't yet glorified. (WEB) *When Jesus cried this out to the crowds in Jerusalem it would have been around the same time that the Temple Priests would have been going down to the Shiloach spring, also called Gihon spring and pool of Shelah, the original source of water for Jerusalem. They would fill up a golden flask with water and bring it back up to the Temple, entering through the Water Gate, on the southern side. As they entered, there would be loud blasts from the shofars and a great shout of celebration would erupt. The water would then be poured out onto the altar of God in the Temple. Remember when Jesus returns to earth, standing on the Mount of Olives, splitting the mountain in two? Keep this in the back of your mind. The landscape will be restructured at Jesus' return, raising up Jerusalem and lowering the land around it. Next, rivers of living water will begin to pour out from Jerusalem, flowing year-round, one part of the river going to the east, the other to the west. There will be much more to talk about this later.*

The Feast of Tabernacles fluctuates on the Gregorian calendar. It can start as early as the latter part of September and end as late as the latter part of October. It is a time to reflect on everything that one possesses due to the blessing of God. Some people *may say it is through my own hard work that I have this and that. However, who gave you the ability to work hard and to think so well? All that we cherish is a gift from God. It will be a time to display the blessings of God as the harvest has already begun for the year in many parts of the world. Yes, if you speak with a farmer, this time period is in the midst of their busiest time of year, their harvest time. For instance, in the United States, depending on where one lives, field corn is harvested anywhere between early September to mid-December. One would probably only want to plant winter barley instead of summer barley as the latter is normally harvested during this time period. Both winter and summer wheat seem to be unaffected by this time period as the time range is flexible. The Soft Red Winter Wheat is the most affected, but could still be done, just in a shorter period of planting time. The oat crop won't be affected much. The most affected crop would be the soybeans. Though one could still work it out. The vegetable crops are pretty much unaffected as they can be worked around. Some areas may not want to plant certain crops, such as the deep southeast of the US' pumpkin crop is during that time. For the fruit crop, cranberries in Maine are the most affected. However, that is looking at today's climate. God is the Creator and He is able to take care of the crops while the farmers are in Jerusalem worshipping Him as it says repeatedly in His Word that it will be after the harvest has been completed that they will come to Jerusalem. It might be that He will change the climate of the earth as He changed the geography of the earth. It will be exciting to see what He does. For those of us who love and serve God as well as those who survive through to the end of the Tribulation Period, we will find out what will happen. It does say in God's Word that if the people do not go, He will not send rain to their fields as His divine judgment upon those who refuse to come. Therefore, that would be devastating. It would be better to go in faith, trusting God for His provisions while one goes to worship Him in Jerusalem. Our God is so good, He will take care of everything. It is quite interesting how well He takes care of everything. With so many people coming to this feast He will make every cooking pot and utensil in all of Jerusalem and Judah, in every household in those parts, holy unto the Lord. Therefore, they will not be guilty of sin before God for boiling any of the meat they are bringing unto God as an offering as well as part of their celebration. Isn't God so good! He thinks of everything, even down to the lowly utensil in your drawer.*

Zechariah 14: 16-21

16 It will happen that everyone (*the totality*) who is left of all the nations that came against Jerusalem will go up from year to year to worship the King, the LORD (Yahweh) of hosts (Tsaba), and to keep (*make the pilgrimage to celebrate with feasting, dancing and festivities*) the feast of booths (*Feast of Tabernacles*). 17 It will be, that whoever of all the families of the earth doesn't go up to Jerusalem to worship the King, the LORD (Yahweh) of hosts (Tsaba), on them there will be no rain. 18 If the family of Egypt doesn't go up and enter in, on them will be the plague (*no rain, severe drought*) with which the LORD (Yahweh) will strike the nations that do not go up to keep the feast of booths. 19 This will be the punishment of Egypt, and the punishment of all the nations that do not go up to keep the feast of booths (*Feast of Tabernacles*). 20 In that day there will be on the bells of the horses,

"HOLY (QODESH) TO THE LORD (YAHWEH);" and the pots (pots used in the sanctuary for boiling and washing) in the LORD's (Yahweh's) house will be like the bowls (*bowls of sprinkling the holy blood of the sacrificed animals*) before the altar. 21 Yes, every pot (*household pots and utensils*) in Jerusalem and in Judah will be holy to the LORD (Yahweh) of hosts (Tsaba); and all those who sacrifice (*slaughter a clean, sacrificial animal for sacrifice unto God*) will come and take of them, and cook (*boil*) in them. In that day there will no longer be a Canaanite (*pre-Israeli inhabitants*) in the house of the LORD (Yahweh) of hosts (Tsaba). (NHEB)

Temple of God,
His Presence in the Land of Israel

You may wonder why the next section is so extensive. I have included it here because God spent many chapters in scripture describing His Temple, which will be built in Jerusalem. Do you recall that Jesus was the son of a carpenter or a stonemason? The Greek word 'tekton' in Matthew 13:55 means a craftsman or builder. Where Jesus lived, most homes were made of stone, brick, and masonry. Wood was not as easily accessible as stone was. Additionally, remember that He is making a place for all of us to dwell with Him? He has spent well over two thousand years on it and counting. On top of all of this, Jesus is the Creator of the entire universe. He is an incredible architect and He does everything for a reason. This is His house, where He will dwell for the thousand years with His people in Jerusalem. He wants all of us to be able to picture it in our heads and see how much He desires to commune with us. I will pretty much leave the chapters from scripture as they are with notes interspersed throughout it. I will include the measurements in the English and Metric systems as cubits are foreign to us. All of these measurements are using the Hebrew Long cubit. There is a difference in measurement between which cubits are used. Even though Ezekiel was in Babylon when the Lord revealed the design of the future Temple to him, he was to tell all the Hebrew people of this vision, not the Babylonian people. Thus, the Hebrew long cubit is what would have been referenced. It is similar to us telling a person who uses the foot to picture something in meters or vice versa. It could be done, but calculations would need to be made in order to picture it accurately in one's head. However, the different cubits are not as dissimilar as the meter and foot are for us. The Babylon Long cubit was 19.8 inches and the Hebrew Long cubit was 20.4 inches. Another cubit used in history was the Egyptian Long cubit, which was 20.6 inches. For more information on how cubits are measured, please see For More Study, 1.

The Temple Area Restored

Ezekiel 40: 1-49

<u>1</u> In the twenty-fifth year of our captivity, in the beginning of the year, in the tenth day of the month, in the fourteenth year after the city was struck, in the same day, Yahweh's hand was on me, and he brought me there. <u>2</u> In the visions of God (Elohim) he brought me into the land of Israel, and set me down on a very high mountain, on which was something like the frame of a city to the south. <u>3</u> He brought me there; and, behold, there was a man whose appearance was like the appearance of bronze, with a line of flax in his hand and a measuring reed; and he stood in the gate. <u>4</u> The man said to me, "Son of man, see with your eyes, and hear with your ears, and set your heart on all that I will show you; for you have been brought here so that I may show them to you. Declare all that you see to the house of Israel."

The East Gate

<u>5</u> Behold, there was a wall on the outside of the house all around, and in the man's hand a measuring reed six cubits long, *(10.2 feet, 3.1 meters)* of a cubit and a hand width each. So he measured the thickness of the building, one reed; and the height, one reed. *(10.2 feet, 3.1 meters each)* <u>6</u> Then he came to the gate which looks toward the east, and went up its steps. He measured the threshold of the gate, one reed wide *(10.2 feet, 3.1 meters)*; and the other threshold, one reed wide *(10.2 feet, 3.1 meters)*. <u>7</u> Every lodge (*guard rooms, side rooms*) was one reed long and one reed wide *(total length and width of the guard rooms are:*

10.2 feet, 3.1 meters by 10.2 feet, 3.1 meters). Between the lodges *(guard rooms, side rooms)* was five cubits *(8.75 feet, 2.7 meters)*. The threshold of the gate by the porch *(covered formal porch, serving as an entryway)* of the gate toward the house *(looking inwards towards the temple)* was one reed *(10.2 feet, 3.1 meters)*. 8 He measured also the porch of the gate toward the house, one reed *(10.2 feet, 3.1 meters)*. 9 Then he measured the porch of the gate, eight cubits *(14 feet, 4.2 meters)*; and its posts, two cubits *(3.5 feet, 1 meter)*; and the porch of the gate was toward the house. 10 The side rooms *(guard rooms, side rooms)* of the gate eastward were three on this side, and three on that side. The three of them were of one measure. The posts had one measure on this side and on that side. 11 He measured the width of the opening of the gate, ten cubits *(18 feet, 5.3 meters wide)*; and the length of the gate, thirteen cubits *(23 feet, 6.9 meters long)*; 12 and a border before the lodges *(guard rooms, side rooms)*, one cubit *(20.4 inches [1.7 feet], .52 meters)* on this side, and a border, one cubit *(20.4 inches [1.7 feet], .52 meters)* on that side; and the side rooms, six cubits on this side, and six cubits on that side *(10.2 square feet, 3.1 square meters = 3.17 feet x 3.17 feet or 0.97 meters x 0.97 meters)*. 13 He measured the gate from the roof of the one side room to the roof of the other, a width of twenty-five cubits *(44 feet, 13 meters)*, door *(also meaning entrance)* against door. 14 He also made posts, sixty cubits *(105 feet, 32 meters)*; and the court reached to the posts, around the gate. 15 From the forefront of the gate at the entrance to the forefront of the inner porch of the gate were fifty cubits *(88 feet, 27 meters)*. 16 There were closed windows (*narrow, latticed window*) to the side rooms, and to their posts within the gate all around, and likewise to the arches. Windows were around inward. Palm trees were on (*decorated*) each post.

The Outer Court

₁₇ Then he brought me into the outer court. *(He was brought through the gateway into the outer courtyard of the Temple.)* Behold, there were rooms (*chambers, small rooms*) and a pavement made for the court all around. Thirty rooms were on the pavement. ₁₈ The pavement was by the side of the gates, corresponding to the length of the gates, even the lower pavement. ₁₉ Then he measured the width from the forefront of the lower gate to the forefront of the inner court (*courtyard*) outside, one hundred cubits *(175 feet, 53 meters)*, both on the east and on the north.

The North Gate

₂₀ He measured the length and width of the gate of the outer court (*courtyard*) which faces toward the north. ₂₁ The lodges (*guard rooms, side rooms*) of it were three on this side and three on that side. Its posts and its arches (*covered formal porch, serving as an entryway*) were the same as the measure of the first gate: its length was fifty cubits, and the width twenty-five cubits *(88 feet, 27 meters long by 44 feet, 13 meters wide)*. ₂₂ Its windows, its arches, and its palm trees were the same as the measure of the gate which faces toward the east. They went up to it by seven steps. Its arches were before them. ₂₃ There was a gate to the inner court (*courtyard*) facing the

other gate, on the north and on the east. He measured one hundred cubits *(175 feet, 53 meters)* from gate to gate.

The South Gate

₂₄ He led me toward the south; and behold, there was a gate toward the south. He measured its posts (*side pillars or posts*) and its arches (*covered formal porch, serving as an entryway*) according to these measurements. ₂₅ There were windows (*narrow, latticed windows*) in it and in its arches all around, like the other windows: the length was fifty cubits, and the width twenty-five cubits *(88 feet, 27 meters long by 44 feet, 13 meters wide)*. ₂₆ There were seven steps to go up to it, and its arches were before them. It had palm trees, one on this side, and another on that side, on its posts. ₂₇ There was a gate to the inner court (courtyard) toward the south. He measured one hundred cubits *(175 feet, 53 meters)* from gate to gate toward the south.

The Gates of the Inner Court

₂₈ Then he brought me to the inner court (*courtyard*) by the south gate. He measured the south gate according to these measurements; ₂₉ with its lodges (*guard rooms, side rooms*), its posts, and its arches (*covered formal porch, serving as an entryway*), according to these measurements. There were windows (*narrow, latticed windows*) in it and in its arches all around. It was fifty cubits long, and twenty-five cubits wide *(88 feet, 27 meters long by 44 feet, 13 meters wide)*. ₃₀ There were arches (*covered formal*

porch, serving as an entryway) all around, twenty-five cubits long and five cubits wide *(44 feet, 13 meters wide by 8.75 feet, 2.7 meters deep)*. ₃₁ Its arches were toward the outer court (*courtyard*). Palm trees were on (*decorated*) its posts. The ascent to it had eight steps. ₃₂ He brought me into the inner court (*courtyard*) toward the east. He measured the gate according to these measurements; ₃₃ with its lodges (*guard rooms, side rooms*), its posts, and its arches (*covered formal porch, serving as an entryway*), according to these measurements. There were windows (*narrow, latticed windows*) in it and in its arches (*covered formal porch, serving as an entryway*) all around. It was fifty cubits long, and twenty-five cubits wide *(88 feet, 27 meters long by 44 feet, 13 meters wide)*. ₃₄ Its arches (*covered formal porch, serving as an entryway*) were toward the outer court (*courtyard*). Palm trees were on (*decorated*) its posts on this side and on that side. The ascent to it had eight steps.

₃₅ He brought me to the north gate, and he measured it according to these measurements— ₃₆ its lodges (*guard rooms, side rooms*), its posts, and its arches (*covered formal porch, serving as an entryway*). There were windows (*narrow, latticed windows*) in it all around. The length was fifty cubits and the width twenty-five cubits *(88 feet, 27 meters long by 44 feet, 13 meters wide)*. ₃₇ Its posts were toward the outer court. Palm trees were on (*decorated*) its posts on this side and on that side. The ascent to it had eight steps.

Eight Tables for Sacrifices

38 A room with its door was by the posts at the gates. They washed the burnt offering there. 39 In the porch of the gate were two tables on this side and two tables on that side, on which to kill the burnt offering, the sin offering, and the trespass offering. 40 On the one side outside, as one goes up to the entry of the gate toward the north, were two tables; and on the other side, which belonged to the porch of the gate, were two tables. 41 Four tables were on this side, and four tables on that side, by the side of the gate: eight tables, on which they killed the sacrifices. 42 There were four cut (hewn) stone tables for the burnt offering, a cubit and a half long, a cubit and a half wide (*2⅔ feet, 80 cm long and wide*), and one cubit high (*21 inches, 53 cm high*). They laid the instruments with which they killed the burnt offering and the sacrifice on them. 43 The hooks, a hand width long (*3.5 inches, 9 cm*), were fastened within all around. The meat of the offering was on the tables.

Rooms for the Priests

44 Outside of the inner gate were rooms for the singers (*Septuagint says: for the singers*) in the inner court (*courtyard*), which was at the side of the north gate. They faced toward the south. One at the side of the east gate faced toward the north. 45 He said to me, "This room, which faces toward the south, is for the priests who perform the duty (*have the responsibility and take care of the temple*) of the house. 46 The room which faces toward the north is for the priests who perform the duty (*keep charge,*

maintain) of the altar. These are the sons of Zadok, who from among the sons of Levi come near to Yahweh to minister to him."

The Inner Courtyard

<u>47</u> He measured the court, one hundred cubits long and one hundred cubits wide, square (*175 feet, 53 meters each length*). The altar was before the house. <u>48</u> Then he brought me to the porch (*covered formal porch, serving as an entryway*) of the house, and measured each post of the porch, five cubits on this side, and five cubits on that side (*8.75 feet, 2.7 meters each side*). The width of the gate was three cubits on this side and three cubits on that side (*5.25 feet, 1.6 meters each side*). <u>49</u> The length of the porch (*covered formal porch, serving as an entryway*) was twenty cubits (*35 feet, 11 meters*) and the width eleven cubits (*21 feet, 6.4 meters*), even by the steps (*10 steps*) by which they went up to it. There were pillars by the posts, one on this side, and another on that side. (WEB)

The Holy Place

Ezekiel 41: 1-26 (1-7)
<u>1</u> He brought me to the nave (*the Holy Place, the outer sanctuary of the temple, as opposed to the inner Holy of Holies*) and measured the posts, six cubits wide on the one side and six cubits (*11 feet, 3.2 meters each*) wide on the other side, which was the width of the tent (*the Holy Place, the outer sanctuary*). <u>2</u> The width of the entrance was ten cubits (*18 feet, 5.3 meters*), and the sides of the entrance were five cubits on the one side, and five cubits on the other side (*8.75 feet,*

2.7 meters each side). He measured its length, forty cubits, and the width, twenty cubits *(70 feet, 21 meters long by 35 feet, 11 meters wide).* (WEB)

Holy of Holies

₃ Then he went inward (*The Holy of Holies*) and measured each post of the entrance, two cubits *(3.5 feet, 1.1 meters)*; and the entrance, six cubits *(11 feet, 3.2 meters)*; and the width of the entrance, seven cubits *(12 feet, 3.7 meters).* ₄ He measured its length, twenty cubits, and the width, twenty cubits *(70 feet, 21 meters length and width)*, before the nave (*Holy Place*). He said to me, "This is the most (*Qodesh*) holy place (*Qodesh*)." (*Holy of Holies*)

₅ Then he measured the wall of the house (*temple*), six cubits *(11 feet, 3.2 meters)*; and the width of every side room, four cubits *(7 feet, 2.1 meters)*, all around the house (*temple*) on every side. ₆ The side rooms were in three stories, one over another, and thirty in each story. They entered into the wall which belonged to the house (*temple*) for the side rooms all around, that they might be supported and not penetrate the wall of the house. (*It appears that from the wall of the Temple, there were areas of the wall thicker than 6 cubits to act as a ledge on which to place the floor of the upper two stories of the side rooms. Thus, there were no supports inserted into the wall projecting out to serve as each of the upper two stories' foundation, rather the one edge of the flooring rested on the ledge of the Temple wall that stuck out to make a ledge all the way around.*) ₇ The side rooms were wider on the higher levels, because the walls were narrower at the higher levels. Therefore the width of the house (*temple*) increased upward; and so one went up from

the lowest level to the highest through the middle level. (WEB)

The picture on the next page is of the stairway and successive floors as it was a little hard for me to imagine it. In this picture, Biblia Prints has it as a cutaway so you may see how it looks. Therefore, it is not shown as enclosed rooms. I believe the walkway for this whole side is along the inner wall. If you go to their website, you will see other pictures with it all enclosed. This picture is from a series of pictures beautifully produced by Biblia Prints showing the Ezekiel chapter 41 temple. I would recommend checking out their website page to view more pictures for your own personal understanding and education.

Ezekiel's vision of the Temple: Part 2 :: Ezekiel's . - FreeBibleimages. Retrieved February 20, 2022, from https://www.freebibleimages.org/illustrations/ezekiel-41-temple/ Used by permission.

Ezekiel 41: 8-26

8 I saw also that the house had a raised base all around. The foundations of the side rooms were a full reed of six great cubits (11 feet, 3.2 meters). *(Most commentators believe this is in reference to the height of each of the side rooms, from floor to ceiling.)* 9 The thickness of the outer wall of the side rooms was five cubits (8.75 feet, 2.7 meters). That which was left was the place of the side rooms that belonged to the house. *(Many commentators understand this to be a walkway.)* 10 Between the rooms was a width of twenty cubits (70 feet, 21 meters) around the house on every side. 11 The doors of the side rooms were toward an open area that was left, one door toward the north, and another door toward the south. The width of the open area (*open walkway*) was five cubits (8.75 feet, 2.7 meters) all around. For more explanation about these rooms and the open walkway, go to For More Study, 2.

12 The building that was before the separate place at the side toward the west was seventy cubits (123 feet, 37 meters) wide; and the wall of the building was five cubits (8.75 feet, 2.7 meters) thick all around, and its length ninety cubits (158 feet, 48 meters).

13 So he measured the temple, one hundred cubits (175 feet, 53 meters) long; and the separate place, and the building, with its walls, one hundred cubits (175 feet, 53 meters) long; 14 also the width of the face of the temple, and of the separate place toward the east, one hundred cubits (175 feet, 53 meters).

15 He measured the length of the building before the separate place which was at its back, and its galleries (*side-rooms or side-chambers*) on the one side and on the other side, one hundred cubits (175 feet, 53

meters) from the inner temple [I believe this means the Holy Place and the Holy of Holies], and the porches of the court, 16 the thresholds, and the closed windows, and the galleries (*side-rooms or side-chambers*) around on their three stories, opposite the threshold, with wood ceilings all around, and from the ground up to the windows, (*now the windows were covered*), 17 to the space above the door, even to the inner house, and outside, and by all the wall all around inside and outside, by measure. 18 It was made with cherubim and palm trees. A palm tree was between cherub and cherub, and every cherub had two faces, 19 so that there was the face of a man toward the palm tree on the one side, and the face of a young lion toward the palm tree on the other side. [*It is so interesting as two of the four faces of the Cherubim shown on the walls reference Jesus, God taking on human flesh and as the Lion of Judah. The palm tree has long been associated with Israel. The trees are usually the first to be seen at a distance to indicate water. Also, it symbolizes beauty, fruitfulness, and righteousness throughout scripture. For information on the palm tree in scripture, please go to For More Study, 3.*] It was made like this through all the house all around. 20 Cherubim and palm trees were made from the ground to above the door. The wall of the temple (*The Temple, Holy Place*) was like this.

21 The door posts [*Some translations say 'posts', but it really means door frame.*] of the nave (*Holy Place*) were squared. As for the face of the nave (*Holy Place*), its appearance was as the appearance of the temple (*Holy of Holies*). 22 The altar was of wood, three cubits (*5.25 feet, 1.5 meters*) high, and its length two cubits (*3.5 feet, 1.1 meters*). Its corners, its base, and its

walls were of wood. (*Most commentators believe this is the Altar of Incense. If so, this is quite telling as it shows how deeply God cherishes our prayers, interacting with Him. [Psalm 141:1-2; Revelation 5:8; 8:3–4, Exodus 30:1-10] From every furniture item in the Holy Place, the Altar of Incense, the piece that signifies our prayers, communion with Him, is chosen to be first mentioned as well as being set up front and center in the Holy of Holies. He so deeply wants to hear everything that we say to Him each and every moment of the day.*) He said to me, "This is the table that is before Yahweh." 23 The temple and the sanctuary had two doors. 24 The doors had two leaves each, two turning leaves: two for the one door, and two leaves for the other. 25 There were made on them, on the doors of the nave, cherubim and palm trees, like those made on the walls. There was a threshold of wood on the face of the porch outside. 26 There were closed windows and palm trees on the one side and on the other side, on the sides of the porch. This is how the side rooms of the temple and the thresholds (*roofs or thick beams*) were arranged. (WEB)

The Rooms for the Priests

Ezekiel 42: 1-20
1 Then he brought me forth into the outer court, the way toward the north: and he brought me into the chamber that was over against the separate place, and which was over against the building toward the north. 2 Before the length of a hundred cubits *(175 feet, 53 meters)* was the north door, and the breadth was fifty cubits *(88 feet, 27 meters)*. 3 Over against the twenty cubits *(35 feet, 11 meters)* which belonged to the inner court, and over against the pavement which

belonged to the outer court, was gallery [*I believe this was the walkway or passageway on the three sides of the temple leading to the chambers*] against gallery in the third story (*each of the three stories*). 4 And before the chambers was a walk of ten cubits *(18 feet, 5.3 meters)* breadth inward, a way of one cubit; [*Some translations say a hundred cubits long instead of one cubit.*] and their doors were toward the north. 5 Now the upper chambers were shorter; for the galleries took away from these, more than from the lower and the middlemost, in the building. 6 For they were in three stories, and they had not pillars as the pillars of the courts: therefore the uppermost was straitened more than the lowest and the middlemost from the ground. 7 And the wall that was without by the side of the chambers, toward the outer court before the chambers, the length thereof was fifty cubits (88 feet, 27 meters). 8 For the length of the chambers that were in the outer court was fifty cubits (88 feet, 27 meters): and, lo, before the temple were a hundred cubits (175 feet, 53 meters). 9 And from under these chambers was the entry on the east side, as one goeth into them from the outer court.

10 In the thickness of the wall of the court toward the east, before the separate place, and before the building, there were chambers. 11 And the way before them was like the appearance of the way of the chambers which were toward the north; according to their length so was their breadth: and all their egresses were both according to their fashions, and according to their doors. 12 And according to the doors of the chambers that were toward the south was a door at the head of the way, even the way

directly before the wall toward the east, as one entereth into them.

₁₃ Then said he unto me, The north chambers and the south chambers, which are before the separate place, they are the holy chambers, where the priests that are near unto Jehovah (Yahweh) shall eat the most holy things: there shall they lay the most holy things, and the meal-offering, and the sin-offering, and the trespass-offering; for the place is holy. ₁₄ When the priests enter in, then shall they not go out of the holy place into the outer court, but there they shall lay their garments wherein they minister; for they are holy: and they shall put on other garments, and shall approach to that which pertaineth to the people. [*This follows Leviticus chapter 16 when Aaron and any succeeding high priest goes in to present the sin offering of atonement. He is to bathe before putting on the holy garments, next perform the sacrifice, then bathe again before putting on regular garments as this is a holy service. More is explained regarding this in Ezekiel 44: 17-23.*]

Ezekiel 42: 15-20

₁₅ Now when he had made an end of measuring the inner house, he brought me forth by the way of the gate whose prospect is toward the east, and measured it round about. ₁₆ He measured on the east side with the measuring reed five hundred reeds (875 feet, 265 meters), with the measuring reed round about. ₁₇ He measured on the north side five hundred reeds (875 feet, 265 meters) with the measuring reed round about. ₁₈ He measured on the south side five hundred reeds (875 feet, 265 meters) with the measuring reed. ₁₉ He turned about to the west side, and measured five hundred reeds (875 feet, 265 meters) with the measuring reed. [20] He measured it on the four sides: it had a wall round about, the length five hundred, and the breadth five hundred (about 5.7 acres, 2.3 hectares), to make a separation between that which was holy and that which was common. (NHEB)

God's Glory Returns to the Temple

In Ezekiel chapters 10 and 11:17-25, during Ezekiel's lifetime, he watched as the Lord's presence and His glory left the former Temple going eastward due to the corruption and iniquity of the Israelites. Now, in these chapters he watches as the presence of God returns to the Millennial Temple. The Lord's presence fills this Temple just as He had filled the Tabernacle in the wilderness and the first Temple that Israel built in the past. These instances were recorded in Exodus 40: 33-38, I Kings 8:1-11, and II Chronicles 7:1-6. As I read about this, it has come to my attention that God's presence never came to fill the Second Temple, except when Jesus was in it. I discovered this while looking through Ezra 6: 13-22, Luke 2:22-52, John 2:13-25, 7:14-30, 8:1-20, Mark 11: 1-11, and Matthew 21:14-17. Additionally, I took a look at the Third Temple built during the Tribulation Period, Revelation chapter 11. It, too, was never filled with God's presence as the Tabernacle and the first Temple were. The Two Witnesses minister outside of the earthly Third Temple, while God's Temple with His presence remains in Heaven during this time period. The Antichrist comes in to occupy the earthly Third Temple. You may see this in Daniel 9:27, Matthew 24:15-25, and II Thessalonians 2:1-12.

The Lord speaks to Ezekiel and says that the place where He sets His feet will never again be made unclean. Neither by Israel or Israel's kings by their prostitution and dead body offerings made for their kings at their death. Israel will not put a wall between Elohim and them, defiling Yahweh's holy name by their abominable practices. One of the things that an abomination is in scripture is labeling what is bad in God's eyes as being good and what is good in God's eyes as being bad. It is twisting the truth. I read a number of the commentators on what dead body offerings the past kings of Israel had or what carcasses there were as this word might also be translated as that here. Most agree that it is in reference to the idolatrous practices of the Israeli kings, some even setting up the lifeless idols in the Temple itself. Unfortunately, Mannasseh, King of Judah, was completely opposite of his father Hezekiah who loved the Lord God. Mannasseh hated the Lord and defiled the Temple of Yahweh by putting numerous idols and altars in the Temple as shown in II Kings 21: 1-15. One of those gods was Molech/Molek where people would bring their infants or young children and sacrifice them on the burning arms of the idol. This is sadly addressed throughout the Bible, such as Leviticus 18:21, Leviticus 20:1-5, I Kings 11:1-13, II Kings 23:1-20, and Jeremiah 32:26-35. If I may be so bold, this false god is still worshipped by many people through abortions, sacrificing their children for their goals in life. However, realize there is forgiveness from God for this. He loves you, even in the pain that follows from this action. Realize the love God has for you is shown in giving His only Son, Jesus, for you so that He might draw you back to Himself and wrap His arms around you in love. Another example of defiling Yahweh's Temple is when He showed Ezekiel some of the idolatrous practices occurring in the Temple itself, hidden behind a wall in Ezekiel chapter eight. Barnes Commentary speaks of Solomon's Palace abutting the southern side of the Temple Mound embankment. Also, one might read into what is said here in II Kings 21, verses 18 and 26 about the "the garden of Uzza" where Manasseh and Amon were buried as well as other Jewish burial sites in the Kidron Valley on the west side of the Mount of Olives as they await the coming Messiah from the east. Then, in the present day, the Muslims have set up a burial ground on the eastern part of the Temple Mound. If you would like to read more about this, go to For More Study, 4. This area will have already been restructured and rebuilt as mentioned previously in Jeremiah 31: 38-40, Zechariah 14: 6-11 as well as all of the rebuilding of the Temple as aforementioned. Moreover, the Dome of the Rock, Qubbat al-Sakrah, that is built on the Temple Mount will have collapsed alongside the rebuilt Third Temple due to the horrific earthquake that will hit the area as the landscape of the region is restructured.

    Elohim, the Triune God who is the One and only True God, Creator of all that exists will come to fill His Temple. His glory will be radiant, filling the land with His glorious light. Can you even imagine what that day will be like? The incredible manifest presence of God coming in all of His glory and majesty. The intense holiness, the intense love of God, more than humans can even comprehend coming into the Temple, His home with us. We all shall fall face down in worship before our magnificent God. When He speaks, it will sound like the roar of a mighty, thundering river. As He faithfully keeps His covenants, He will renew His guarantee that this is where He will remain among the Israelites forever. We will never again know a time that He is not right here in the midst of us. We will forever be in His glorious presence. After Elohim's presence enters into the Temple through the eastern gate, that *gate will not to be opened again, except for special occasions since the Lord Himself entered in through that gate. The eastern gate will only be opened when the prince sits in the gateway of the eastern gate to eat in the presence of Yahweh. He is to enter the gate, eat, and then go back out the way in which he entered.*

Ezekiel 43: 1-12

1 Afterward he brought me to the gate, even the gate that looks toward the east. 2 Behold, the glory of the God (Elohim) of Israel came from the way of the east. His voice was like the sound of many waters; and the earth was illuminated with his glory. 3 It was like the appearance of the vision which I saw, even according to the vision that I saw when I came to destroy the city; and the visions were like the vision that I saw by the river Chebar; and I fell on my face. 4 Yahweh's glory came into the house by the way of the gate which faces toward the east. 5 The Spirit (Ruach) took me up and brought me into the inner court; and behold, Yahweh's glory filled the house.

6 I heard one speaking to me out of the house, and a man stood by me. 7 He said to me, "Son of man (Adam), this is the place of my throne and the place of the soles of my feet, where I will dwell among the children of Israel forever. The house of Israel will no more defile my holy name, neither they nor their kings, by their prostitution and by the dead bodies of their kings in their high places; 8 in their setting of their threshold by my threshold and their door post beside my door post. There was a wall between me and them; and they have defiled my holy name by their abominations which they have committed. Therefore I have consumed them in my anger. 9 Now let them put away their prostitution, and the dead bodies of their

kings far from me. Then I will dwell among them forever.

10 "You, son of man, show the house to the house of Israel, that they may be ashamed of their iniquities; and let them measure the pattern. 11 If they are ashamed of all that they have done, make known to them the form of the house, its fashion, its exits, its entrances, its structure, all its ordinances, all its forms, and all its laws; and write it in their sight, that they may keep the whole form of it, and all its ordinances, and do them. 12 "This is the law of the house. On the top of the mountain the whole limit around it shall be most holy. Behold, this is the law of the house. (WEB)

Ezekiel 44: 1-3

1 Then he brought me back by the way of the outer gate of the sanctuary, which looks toward the east; and it was shut. 2 Yahweh said to me, "This gate shall be shut. It shall not be opened, no man shall enter in by it; for Yahweh, the God (Elohim) of Israel, has entered in by it. Therefore it shall be shut. 3 As for the prince, he shall sit in it as prince to eat bread before Yahweh. He shall enter by the way of the porch of the gate, and shall go out the same way."

Healing Water of God That Flows From the Temple

When one looks at the entrance to the Temple of God itself, which front faces east, water is seen coming from under the south, the left side, of the Temple. The Altar of Burnt Offering, which will be spoken of later, is to the north of the of the river, because the river turns eastward after leaving the temple. The water flows continuously, like water boiling over or like a natural spring continually bubbling up. Ezekiel is led out of the north gate to go to the east side as the eastern gate is closed on working days. As he turns back to look at the eastern gate, the river is seen to the left of the gate, south of it as the river continues to flow eastward. After he walks from the outer wall 1,700 feet, .32 mile, 518 meters or .52 KM the river becomes knee-deep in depth. Then after traversing another .32 miles or .52 KM the water is now waist deep. Then another .32 miles or .52 KM the river is now a rushing river; over one's head in depth. A person can no longer gain a footing to cross it, but has to swim. So, in almost one mile or 1.6 KM the river goes from a trickle to a river too deep to cross on foot.

On each side of the river, there will be numerous trees, especially fruit trees. These trees will bear fruit monthly due to the healing qualities of the water that will flow from the Temple of God. Its fruit will be edible and the trees' leaves will be used for their healing qualities. As the river flows into the desert valley of the Jordan River entering the Dead Sea, the waters will heal the Dead Sea. It will turn the Dead Sea into a body of freshwater enabling abundant life to return to it. There will be a great abundance of fish, like the great diversity of life found in the Mediterranean Sea. From En Gedi to En Eglaim fishermen will spread their nets.

En Gedi is midway down the coast on the west side of the Dead Sea. En Eglaim is not fully known. Some commentators put it at the east side of the entrance of the Jordan River. Some other commentators put it on the east side farther down the coast in Moab, which is presently the country of Jordan. Either way, the entire upper coastland or the entire breadth of the Sea will have abundant life. The swamps and marshes, probably on the southern end of the Dead Sea will be left brackish for the life that is currently found in the Dead Sea to remain as well as for the collection of salt. Currently, even in the extreme salinity levels of the Dead Sea some bacteria, such as cyanobacteria and green sulfur bacteria, microscopic algae, such as Dunaliella algae, and eighty different species of fungi live in the water. Along its edge at our present time there are animals, such as some river crabs and snails, marsh frogs, European green toads, along with a variety of water insects.

Other prophets of God also spoke of this river. Joel 3:18 [18] *It will happen in that day, that the mountains will drop down sweet wine, the hills will flow with milk, all the brooks of Judah will flow with waters, and a fountain will come forth from the house of Yahweh, and will water the valley of Shittim.* (WEB) *Zechariah 14:8* [8] *It will happen in that day, that living waters will go out from Jerusalem; half of them toward the eastern sea, and half of them toward the western sea; in summer and in winter will it be.* (WEB) *There will be a similar river to the one flowing from the Temple of God that Ezekiel saw, but this future one will be found in New Jerusalem. This future river will also be a healing and life giving river as described in* Revelation 22: 1-2 ₁ He showed me a river of water of life, clear as crystal, proceeding out of the throne of God and of the Lamb, ₂ in the middle of its street. On this side of the river and on that was the tree of life, bearing twelve kinds of fruits, yielding its fruit every month. The leaves of the tree were for the healing of the nations. (NHEB) *The river during the Millennium is a forerunner to the eternal river in New Jerusalem.*

Ezekiel 47: 1-12
₁ He brought me back to the door of the house; and behold, waters issued out from under the threshold of the house eastward; (*for the forefront of the house was toward the east;*) and the waters came down from under, from the right side of the house, on the south of the altar. ₂ Then he brought me out by the way of the gate northward, and led me round by the way outside to the outer gate, by the way of [the gate] that looks toward the east; and behold, there ran out waters on the right side.
₃ When the man went forth eastward with the line in his hand, he measured one thousand cubits (about 1,700 feet ⅓ mile, 530 meters), and he caused me to pass through the waters, waters that were to the ankles. ₄ Again he measured one thousand (about .32 mile or .46 km), and caused me to pass through the waters, waters that were to the knees. Again he measured one thousand (about .32 mile or .46 km), and caused me to pass through [the waters], waters that were to the waist. ₅ Afterward he measured one

thousand (about .32 mile or .46 km); [*and it was*] a river that I could not pass through; for the waters were risen, waters to swim in, a river that could not be passed through. 6 He said to me, Son of man (Adam), have you seen [*this*]? Then he brought me, and caused me to return to the bank of the river. 7 Now when I had returned, behold, on the bank of the river were very many trees on the one side and on the other. 8 Then he said to me, These waters issue forth toward the eastern region, and shall go down into the Arabah; and they shall go toward the sea; into the sea [shall the waters go] which were made to issue forth; and the waters shall be healed. 9 It shall happen, that every living creature which swarms, in every place where the rivers come, shall live; and there shall be a very great multitude of fish; for these waters are come there, and [the waters of the sea] shall be healed, and everything shall live wherever the river comes. 10 It shall happen, that fishermen shall stand by it: from En Gedi even to En Eglaim shall be a place for the spreading of nets; their fish shall be after their kinds, as the fish of the great sea, exceeding many. 11 But the miry places of it, and its marshes, shall not be healed; they shall be given up to salt. 12 By the river on its bank, on this side and on that side, shall grow every tree for food, whose leaf shall not wither, neither shall its fruit fail: it shall bring forth new fruit every month, because its waters issue out of the sanctuary; and its fruit shall be for food, and its leaf for healing. (WEB)

The Great Altar Restored

The Altar of Burnt Offerings will be re-established in the Temple of God. As the sacrifices to God in the Old Testament had the people look towards the sacrifice of God's only Son for the forgiveness of our sins, these sacrifices have us looking back to what Jesus did for us on the cross. It is a commemorative act. Young bulls are used for the offerings of purification from sins. The Levitical priests of the family of Zadok are the only ones allowed to minister before Yahweh in these sacrifices as they are the only members of the Levitical family to keep themselves pure from the idolatrous practices that Israel fell into during the past. These sacrifices offered on the Altar of Burnt Offerings will be pleasing to God.

Ezekiel 43:13-27
13 "These are the measurements of the altar by cubits (*the cubit is a cubit and a hand width*) (21 inches, 53 centimeters): the bottom [*other translations say 'gutter'*] shall be a cubit, and the width a cubit, and its border around its edge [*other translations say 'rim'*] a span (11 inches, 27 centimeters); and this shall be the base [*other translations say 'height'*] of the altar. 14 From the bottom on the ground to the lower ledge (*step*) shall be two cubits (3 ½ feet, 105 centimeters), and the width one cubit (1 ¾ feet, 53 centimeters); and from the lesser ledge (*step*) to the greater ledge (*step*) shall be four cubits (7 feet, 2.1 meters), and the width a cubit (1 ¾ feet, 53 centimeters). 15 The upper altar shall be four cubits (7 feet, 2.1 meters); and from the altar hearth and upward there shall be four horns. 16 The altar hearth shall be twelve cubits (21

feet, 6.4 meters) long by twelve (21 feet, 6.4 meters) wide, square in its four sides. 17 The ledge shall be fourteen cubits (25 feet, 7.4 meters) long by fourteen (25 feet, 7.4 meters) wide in its four sides; and the border about it shall be half a cubit (11 inches, 27 centimeters); and its bottom shall be a cubit (1 ¾ feet, 53 centimeters) around; and its steps shall look toward the east."

18 He said to me, "Son of man (Adam), the Lord (Adonai) Yahweh says: 'These are the ordinances of the altar in the day when they make it, to offer burnt offerings on it, and to sprinkle blood on it. 19 You shall give to the Levitical priests who are of the offspring of Zadok, who are near to me, to minister to me,' says the Lord (Adonai) Yahweh, 'a young bull for a sin offering. 20 You shall take of its blood and put it on its four horns, and on the four corners of the ledge, and on the border all around. You shall cleanse it and make atonement for it that way. 21 You shall also take the bull of the sin offering, and it shall be burned in the appointed place of the house, outside of the sanctuary.

22 "On the second day you shall offer a male goat without defect for a sin offering; and they shall cleanse the altar, as they cleansed it with the bull. 23 When you have finished cleansing it, you shall offer a young bull without defect and a ram out of the flock without defect. 24 You shall bring them near to Yahweh, and the priests shall cast salt on them, and they shall offer them up for a burnt offering to Yahweh. 25 "Seven days you shall prepare every day a goat for a sin offering. They shall also prepare a young bull and a ram out of the flock, without defect. 26 Seven days shall they make atonement for

the altar and purify it. So shall they consecrate it. 27 When they have accomplished the days, it shall be that on the eighth day and onward, the priests shall make your burnt offerings on the altar and your peace offerings. Then I will accept you,' says the Lord (Adonai) Yahweh." (WEB)

The Priesthood Restored

The defilement of the priesthood will be done away with during the millennial period of time. In previous times, foreigners, those who were uncircumcised in heart and flesh came into the Temple in Israel to present sacrifices. This reminds me of Revelation 22: 13-15 where Jesus says: 13 I am the Alpha and the Omega, the First and the Last, the Beginning and the End. 14 Blessed are they who wash their robes, that they may have the right to the tree of life, and may enter in by the gates into the city. 15 Outside are the dogs, the sorcerers, the sexually immoral, the murderers, the idolaters, and everyone who loves and practices falsehood. (NHEB) *Those who are not allowed into the city of God and partake of its benefits are those who are of uncircumcised hearts, who have not been cleansed by the blood of Jesus. The priesthood in the past put others in charge of doing the work they were supposed to do, defiling the Temple of God. They were not guarding His Temple or keeping the Sabbaths and appointed feasts holy among the people. We, who follow Christ Jesus, are the Temple of God as the Holy Spirit indwells each of us, individually. As I Corinthians 3: 16-20 says:* 16 Don't you know that you are a temple of God, and that God's Spirit lives in you? 17 If anyone destroys the temple of God, God will destroy him; for God's temple is holy, which you are. 18 Let no one deceive himself. If anyone thinks that he is wise among you in this world, let him become a fool, that he may become wise. 19 For the wisdom of this world is foolishness with God. For it is written, "He has taken the wise in their craftiness." 20 And again, "The Lord knows the reasoning of the wise, that it is worthless." (WEB) *We are to guard what comes into our thoughts, taking every thought captive. We are to be careful in not allowing ourselves to become defiled by taking thoughts from the evil one, the enemy of our soul, and placing them into our hearts and minds as something to keep. As II Corinthians 10: 3-5 says:* 3 For though we walk in the flesh, we do not wage war according to the flesh; 4 for the weapons of our warfare are not of the flesh, but mighty in God for the tearing down of strongholds, 5 throwing down imaginations and every high thing that is exalted against the knowledge of God, and bringing every thought into captivity to the obedience of Christ; (NHEB) *We need to put every teaching, philosophy, doctrine, and cultural understanding through the filter of God's Word. Does it align with God's Word or not? If it does not line up with God's Word or the characteristics of who God has shown Himself to be in His word, then do not adopt it into your life. If it does, accept it and keep it close to your heart. The people of Israel in the past, especially a large number of the Levites and priests had put idols and stumbling blocks into the paths of the people of Israel causing them to go astray from serving Yahweh. There are consequences to their actions that have gone down through the generations. That is why only the descendants of Zadok may serve in the presence of God. One of the first mentions of Zadok is found in I Chronicles 6:8. Zadok was a co-high priest with Abiathar during the time of David. He was a descendant of Aaron, the leader over the descendants of Aaron of the Tribe of Levi as noted in I Chronicles 27:17. In II Samuel 15: 13-14, 17:16 and 18:1-15 it describes how he supported David when he was on the run from his son Absalom and sent him news of what was happening, protecting him as well as receiving him back in victory. Then again in I Kings chapter one it describes how Zakok supported both David and Solomon when David's son Adonijah tried to take the throne of David. He served as the high priest along with Abiathar under Solomon's time in I Kings 4:4. Abiathar served a brief period as high priest under Solomon, thus to honor his short tenure, he is listed in 4:4. Abiathar was deposed from his duties in I Kings 2:27, 35. The Zadokites were faithful in serving Yahweh, not ethically led astray or seduced under the deceit of their time. They remained faithful,* מִשְׁמַרְתִּי שָׁמְרוּ *in the function as a priest guarding over what God has prescribed. They preserved the sacredness of Adonai Yahweh's Temple even in the midst of all the idolatry going on in the land and people of Israel. They remained steadfast in their devotion to Yahweh. The other Levites may only serve at the gates of the Temple and work in the slaughtering of the sacrifices. However, they are not to approach Yahweh's presence in offering the sacrifices. Thankfully, because of Jesus' shed blood for us on the cross, each of us, individually, who have accepted His punishment for us on the cross in our place, receiving Him as our Lord and Savior are able to enter Yahweh's presence with confidence as the blood of Christ covers us personally. It says this in Hebrews 4: 14-16.* [14] *Having then a great high priest who has passed through the heavens, Jesus, the Son of God, let's hold tightly to our confession.* [15] *For we don't have a high priest who can't be touched with the feeling of our infirmities, but one who has been in all points tempted like we are, yet without sin.* [16] *Let's therefore draw near with boldness to the throne of* grace, that we may receive mercy and may find grace for help in time of need. (WEB) *Thank you, Jesus, for this tremendous gift You have given to us! The priesthood diligently protects the Temple and holy places of God in Jerusalem. We, the people of God saved through the blood of Christ Jesus will have open access to Yahweh's presence, able to come and go as we desire and/or need. We may approach His Throne without hesitancy and we will be warmly welcomed. Words cannot express how thankful I am to You, Jesus.*

It is interesting for me to read what the priests are to wear. The thought of linen hasn't been appealing to me as for some reason when I picture linen I think of a tablecloth or something bulky and unappealing to wear. So, I looked it up to see how it compares to cotton, for I like to wear cotton to keep myself cool. I was surprised by what I found. For a bed sheet, cotton is good for winter, but may cause a person to overheat during the night. Linen will allow a person's body to breathe through the whole night, so one does not overheat. Linen is considerably stronger and more durable than cotton. Linen is actually a finer cloth than cotton, which surprised me. It is not as fine as silk, but in the middle, between cotton and silk. However, linen wrinkles a lot, much more than cotton does. Also, the cost of linen is considerably higher than cotton, which is why linen is not seen much in clothing. Linen is the kind of cloth that God tells the priests to wear, primarily for the quality of keeping the wearer of it cool. While working, the person does not sweat as one does while wearing wool. Their linen clothes are holy unto God as they have been dedicated to His service. If you recall the three stories of rooms along the sides of the Temple described in Ezekiel chapter 42 is where these garments are stored and where the Priests change their clothes. This is where holy items to the Lord are to be kept, such as the donations given to the Lord. They are kept in these rooms as holy. The priests are not to wear these holy linen clothes worn in service to God outside of the designated areas of the Temple. The reason for this is in case they were to accidentally touch someone not holy, causing the death of that touched person. That accidentally touched person may have done something unholy and has not yet been forgiven of it. Maybe that person is there bringing a sacrifice, but has not yet offered it. I believe this is out of the mercy of God that they are to be careful in where they wear these clothes. If a person comes in contact with these clothes and were to become holy before God without realizing it and then sinned, they would be guilty, thus needing to be put to death. Holiness and unholiness cannot coexist. Unholiness is immediately removed. An example of this is found in II Samuel 6:1-6. I believe a New Testament example of this is found in Acts 5:1-13 with Ananias and Sapphira.

*   God reiterates what He told the priesthood to do as found in Leviticus chapter 21. They are not to shave their heads bare or in the form of designs. In the same light, they are not to grow their hair long. One of the reasons for these prohibitions is that these haircuts are a cultural signal to others that you are in a season of mourning. Also, shaving one's head is what some of the heathen did in serving their gods, such as in Egypt, for their idols Serapis and Isis. The only time long hair was truly deemed allowed by God for men was in respect to the Nazarite vow, to be set apart from other*

people and to be consecrated to God for His service. It could be a vow that is kept for a week or up to a lifetime. Samson, Samuel, and John the Baptist are three examples of people who were under a Nazarite vow. God spoke to their parents that their child would be under such a lifetime vow. (For more information regarding this, read Judges chapter one, I Samuel 1:9-28, and Luke 1:5-23.) When their Nazarite vow is completed, they would then cut their hair and sacrifice it to God as part of a burnt offering. For information on what entails a Nazarite vow, read Numbers 6:1-21. Other guidelines for the priests are that they are not to drink any wine when they are ministering to the Lord. When they marry, they may only marry Israeli virgins or widows of priests. They may not marry any other widows or any divorced persons. They may not go near a person who has died unless that person is of their immediate family. If that happens, they have to wait seven days before coming back to minister before God. Many of God's laws are to protect people. That is why they have to wait seven days. In case the person died of any transmittable disease or illness, symptoms should show up in the person exposed to it normally within a week. Their ministry to the people are multi-faceted. They are to offer up a person's offering to God. They are also to instruct the people how to discern the difference between what is holy and what is for common use, including what is ceremonially pure versus impure. Another one of their job descriptions is to act as a lawyer. They are to settle disputes between people by deciding what should be done according to the laws of God.

Ezekiel 44: 4-31

₄ Then he brought me by the way of the north gate before the house; and I looked, and behold, Yahweh's glory filled Yahweh's house; so I fell on my face. ₅ Yahweh said to me, "Son of man (Adam), mark well, and see with your eyes, and hear with your ears all that I tell you concerning all the ordinances of Yahweh's house and all its laws; and mark well the entrance of the house, with every exit of the sanctuary. ₆ You shall tell the rebellious, even the house of Israel, 'The Lord (Adonai) Yahweh says: "You house of Israel, let that be enough of all your abominations, ₇ in that you have brought in foreigners, uncircumcised in heart and uncircumcised in flesh, to be in my sanctuary, to profane it, even my house, when you offer my bread, the fat and the blood; and they have broken my covenant, to add to all your abominations. ₈ You have not performed the duty of my holy things; but you have set performers of my duty in my sanctuary for yourselves."

₉ The Lord (Adonai) Yahweh says, "No foreigner, uncircumcised in heart and uncircumcised in flesh, shall enter into my sanctuary, of any foreigners who are among the children of Israel. ₁₀ ""But the Levites who went far from me when Israel went astray, who went astray from me after their idols, they will bear their iniquity. ₁₁ Yet they shall be ministers in my sanctuary, having oversight at the gates of the house, and ministering in the house. They shall kill the burnt offering and the sacrifice for the people, and they shall stand before them to minister to them. ₁₂ Because they ministered to them before their idols, and became a stumbling block of iniquity to the house of Israel, therefore I have lifted up my hand (taken an oath) against them," says the Lord (Adonai) Yahweh, "and they will bear their iniquity. 13 They shall not come near to me, to execute the office of priest to me, nor to come near to any of my holy things, to the things that are most holy; but they will bear their shame and their abominations which they have committed. 14 Yet I will make them performers of the duty of the house, for all its service and for all that will be done therein.

15 """But the Levitical priests, the sons of Zadok, who performed the duty of my sanctuary when the children of Israel went astray from me, shall come near to me to minister to me. They shall stand before me to offer to me the fat and the blood," says the Lord (Adonai) Yahweh. 16 "They shall enter into my sanctuary (*Holy Place*), and they shall come near to my table, to minister to me, and they shall keep my instruction. 17 """It will be that when they enter in at the gates of the inner court, they shall be clothed with linen garments. No wool shall come on them while they minister in the gates of the inner court, and within. 18 They shall have linen turbans (*headdress*) on their heads, and shall have linen trousers on their waists. They shall not clothe themselves with anything that makes them sweat. 19 When they go out into the outer court, even into the outer court to the people, they shall put off their garments in which they minister and lay them in the holy rooms. They shall put on other garments, that they not sanctify (*treat as holy*) the people with their garments. 20 """They shall not shave their heads, or allow their locks to grow long. They shall only cut off the hair of their heads. 21 None of the priests shall drink wine when they enter into the inner court. 22 They shall not take for their wives a widow, or her who

is put away; but they shall take virgins of the offspring of the house of Israel, or a widow who is the widow of a priest. 23 They shall teach my people the difference between the holy and the common, and cause them to discern between the unclean and the clean. 24 "'"In a controversy they shall stand to judge. They shall judge it according to my ordinances. They shall keep my laws and my statutes in all my appointed feasts. They shall make my Sabbaths holy. 25 "'"They shall go in to no dead person to defile themselves; but for father, or for mother, or for son, or for daughter, for brother, or for sister who has had no husband, they may defile themselves. 26 After he is cleansed, they shall reckon to him seven days. 27 In the day that he goes into the sanctuary, into the inner court, to minister in the sanctuary, he shall offer his sin offering," says the Lord (Adonai) Yahweh.
28 "'They shall have an inheritance: I am their inheritance; and you shall give them no possession in Israel. I am their possession. 29 They shall eat the meal offering, and the sin offering, and the trespass offering; and every devoted thing in Israel shall be theirs. 30 The first of all the first fruits of every thing, and every offering of everything, of all your offerings, shall be for the priest. You shall also give to the priests the first of your dough, to cause a blessing to rest on your house. 31 The priests shall not eat of anything that dies of itself or is torn, whether it is bird or animal. (WEB)

Adonai Yahweh is going to deal with and end every maltreatment done to His people by His own people in the past. This, I believe, is where we who will reign with Christ during the thousand-year period will be doing wherever we are assigned. Yahweh will not allow any of the princes or those in authority over others to devastate anyone. We, as His ambassadors will deal swiftly with this. The priesthood and we will deal with each person according to the Law of God and do what is ethically righteous. Additionally, the right measurements shall be used by every person. There is not to be any price gouging or favoritism. The weights used in scripture are what they were accustomed to using in Ezekiel's time. The same intent of this rule would apply to what weights we are accustomed to using in our lives. With the biblical weights, one has to understand that a Homer is different from an Omer. The Homer is 10 Ephahs, whereas an Omer is a tenth part of an Ephah. An Ephah is a dry measure, whereas a Bath is a liquid measurement. One Homer worth of grain, still on its stalks is large enough to be bundled. This is similar to how farmers used to harvest their grain decades and centuries ago. The Amish still follow this practice. For more information on this, see For More Study, 5. The Homer, Ephah/Bath and Omer measurements are almost similar to the metric system of today in that they dealt with tens and tenths. The Barnes Notes on the Bible and the Pulpit Commentary estimate a Homer to be about 75 gallons, 32 pecks or 284 liters. However, Biblehub.com shows different measurements. I have used the equivalent measurements found on Biblehub.com. Such measurements are also mentioned in Exodus 36:15-36 and Leviticus 27:16-21. According to the Jamieson-Fausset-Brown Bible Commentary, they say that the standard weights used in the Temple were most probably lost when the Chaldeans destroyed the Temple. There might have been three different enumerations of the Shekel back then of 25, 20 and 15, which when added together would equal one Mina. I will put notations right in the following scripture for the measurements to help keep it understandable in today's terms.

When the people come to God's Temple to present guilt or sin offerings they are not to go into the outer court of the Temple, lest they be made holy and God needs to strike them dead due to bringing sin into a holy place. They are to offer up their offering to the priests, who then will take it in at the extreme western end of the outer court area. They are to boil the guilt and sin offering and bake the grain offering in one of the four corners of the outer court. These areas will be 70 feet/21 meters long and 53 feet/16 meters wide. There will be rows of stone ledges in these corner areas for cooking hearths dedicated to these offerings. For an illustration of how the cooking areas, outer court as well as the whole Temple layout looks, see For More Study, 6.

The people of Israel and the prince are to work as a team to provide special offerings to the Lord. Instead of the prince in the past taking advantage of the people, they are rather to support each other. This has been Yahweh's intent all along through history for each person to be a support to each other, including when Elohim created Eve for Adam. They were to work as a team, supporting each other. As God called Eve a suitable helpmate for Adam, she would come alongside to help him so he would not be all alone. A helpmate is one who is another person's equal so that person would not be above or below, but working side by side.

Remember how previous to Eve being created that God brought all the animals He had created for Adam to name them? From all the animals created, there was not a suitable helpmate found for him. If you would like to refresh your memory, read Genesis chapter two. Elohim wanted to emphasize the fact that no animal could ever take the place of human companionship. Elohim has made us one for another to support each other in positive ways. This is one reason why the people of Israel are to donate the special offerings listed in scripture to the Lord, giving them to the prince for God's use. Then the prince is to offer up these special offerings from the people along with what he is to contribute to the weekly and monthly offerings. On top of all of this, he is to contribute from his own resources what is to be used during the pilgrim feasts, such as Passover and the other annual appointed festivals unto the Lord. The prince is to provide all of the sin offerings, grain offerings, whole burnt offerings, and fellowship offerings for all the people during these times to cover over the sins of the entirety of the people. It even focuses on covering the sins of the open-minded in verse twenty of Ezekiel 45 of the original language. Being open-minded in God's Word means to be simple-minded and naive, thus ignorant of the consequences of choices made in life.

The gate to the Inner Court is to be closed for the six working days. However, it will be opened on every Sabbath and New Moon. These days are when the prince offers the sacrifice. He may go up to the gate entrance and worship the Lord. Then he is to return from the way he came. However, on the high festival days, all the people coming to worship the Lord may enter through the north gate to go through and then out the south gate and vice versa. The prince shall do the same as everyone else. I am unsure, but it appears that everyone may enter the inner court of the Temple, where the sacrifices are actually burned unto God on the altar. One may also glimpse into the Temple of God into the Holy Place of the Sanctuary of the Temple as they pass by. Everyone is to go straight through, without turning back from the way they came. It is almost like what we are told as Believers to walk toward the prize that lies ahead of us. We are not to return to our old ways of living as a dog returns to its vomit or a cleaned pig returns to its muddy wallow. Rather, we are to walk in the newness of life that God has given to us in His blessings. Praise Almighty God for His incredible grace and mercy!

Ezekiel 45: 9-25

9 Thus says the Lord (Adonai) Yahweh: Let it suffice you, princes of Israel: remove violence and spoil, and execute justice and righteousness; dispossessing my people, says the Lord (Adonai) Yahweh.

10 You shall have just balances, and a just ephah (*approximately 0.624 bushels, 5 dry gallons, or .022 cubic meter*), and a just bath (*About 5.8 liquid gallons, 22 liters*). 11 The ephah and the bath shall be of one measure, that the bath may contain the tenth part of a homer (*about 58 liquid gallons, 220 liters or 6.25 bushels, 50 dry gallons, 0.22 cubic meters*), and the ephah the tenth part of a homer: its measure shall be after the homer. 12 The shekel (*approximately 11-12 grams of silver or 4.5 grams of gold*) shall be twenty gerahs (*about 0.55 - 0.6 grams of silver or 0.225 grams of gold*). [*One shekel could buy a person the following*

items. One gallon or four liters of olive oil, 0.75 bushels of wheat, or 3.8 bushels of barley. One ox costs about 12.5 shekels. One sheep costs about 2.5 shekels.] Twenty shekels plus twenty-five shekels plus fifteen shekels shall be your mina (*60 shekels: 660 – 720 grams {23.28 – 25.4 ounces} of silver or 270 grams {8.68 troy ounces} of gold. Before the Babylonian captivity one mina was worth about 50 shekels.*) [As a side note, the price of silver and gold does fluctuate. At the current price in 2025, this amount of silver and gold would be cost prohibitive for most people. It's worth must have been much less back then. The way that the mina is determined can be tied to the prophesy in Daniel 5:25, at the fall of Babylon: Mene, Mene, Tekel, Upharsin. Mene is related to the mina – measurement of weight and money. Tekel is related to the shekel – measurement of weight for worth of money. Upharsin is related to dividing up, as with the 20 shekels plus 25 shekels plus 15 shekels needed to make a mina. The Babylon Kingdom was weighed up and found to be short, not adding up to the total needed; thus, it was divided up and given to the Medes and Persians. In the Bible, one shekel was worth about 4 days worth of labor. As another side note, one talent equals 3,000 shekels. Think about the mention of the talent in the New Testament. These are found in Matthew 18: 21-35, 25: 14-30, and alluded to in Luke 16:1-15, emphasis on verses 10-12.] [13] This is the offering that you shall offer: the sixth part of an ephah (*equal to about 3 quarts, 0.08 bushels, 0.64 gallon, or .003 cubic meter*) from a homer of wheat; and you shall give the sixth part of an ephah from a homer of barley; [14] and the set portion of oil, of the bath of oil, the tenth part of a bath out of the cor (*50 liquid gallons, 220 liters*), ten baths, even a homer; (*for ten baths are a homer*) 15 and one lamb of the flock, out of two hundred, from the well-watered pastures of Israel—for a meal offering, and for a burnt offering, and for peace offerings, to make atonement for them, says the Lord (Adonai) Yahweh. 16 All the people of the land shall give to this offering for the prince in Israel. 17 It shall be the prince's part to give the burnt offerings, and the meal offerings, and the drink offerings, in the feasts, and on the new moons, and on the Sabbaths, in all the appointed feasts of the house of Israel: he shall prepare the sin offering, and the meal offering, and the burnt offering, and the peace offerings, to make atonement for the house of Israel.

18 Thus says the Lord (Adonai) Yahweh: In the first [*month*], in the first [*day*] of the month, you shall take a young bull without blemish; and you shall cleanse (*cleanse from the uncleanness of sin*) the sanctuary. 19 The priest shall take of the blood of the sin offering, and put it on the door posts of the house, and on the four corners of the ledge of the altar, and on the posts of the gate of the inner court. 20 So you shall do on the seventh [day] of the month for everyone who errs, and for him who is simple (*ignorant, open-minded*): so you shall make atonement for the house.

21 In the first [*month*], in the fourteenth day of the month, you shall have the Passover, a feast of seven days; unleavened bread shall be eaten. 22 On that day shall the prince prepare for himself and for all the people of the land a bull for a sin offering. 23 The seven days of the feast he shall prepare a burnt offering to Yahweh, seven bulls and seven rams without blemish daily the seven days; and a male goat daily for a sin offering. 24 He shall prepare a meal

offering, an ephah for a bull, and an ephah for a ram, and a hin (*about 0.98 gallons, 3.71 liters*) of oil to an ephah. 25 In the seventh [month], in the fifteenth day of the month, in the feast, shall he do the like the seven days; according to the sin offering, according to the burnt offering, and according to the meal offering, and according to the oil. (WEB)

Ezekiel 46: 1-15, 19-24
1 Thus says the Lord (Adonai) Yahweh: The gate of the inner court that looks toward the east shall be shut the six working days; but on the Sabbath day it shall be opened, and on the day of the new moon it shall be opened. 2 The prince shall enter by the way of the porch of the gate outside, and shall stand by the post of the gate; and the priests shall prepare his burnt offering and his peace offerings (*sacrifice for alliance or friendship, fellowship offering*), and he shall worship at the threshold of the gate: then he shall go forth; but the gate shall not be shut until the evening. 3 The people of the land shall worship at the door of that gate before Yahweh on the Sabbaths and on the new moons. 4 The burnt offering that the prince shall offer to Yahweh shall be on the Sabbath day six lambs without blemish and a ram without blemish; 5 and the meal offering shall be an ephah for the ram, and the meal offering for the lambs as he is able to give, and a hin of oil to an ephah. 6 On the day of the new moon it shall be a young bull without blemish, and six lambs, and a ram; they shall be without blemish: 7 and he shall prepare a meal offering, an ephah for the bull, and an ephah for the ram, and for the lambs according as he is able, and a hin of oil to an ephah. 8 When the prince shall enter, he shall go in by the way

of the porch of the gate, and he shall go forth by its way. 9 But when the people of the land shall come before Yahweh in the appointed feasts, he who enters by the way of the north gate to worship shall go forth by the way of the south gate; and he who enters by the way of the south gate shall go forth by the way of the north gate: he shall not return by the way of the gate by which he came in, but shall go forth straight before him. 10 The prince, when they go in, shall go in with of them; and when they go out, he shall go out. 11 In the feasts (*pilgrim feasts*) and in the solemnities the meal offering shall be an ephah for a bull (*young bull*), and an ephah for a ram, and for the lambs as he is able to give, and a hin of oil (*olive oil*) to an ephah. 12 When the prince shall prepare a freewill offering, a burnt offering or peace offerings as a freewill offering to Yahweh, one shall open for him the gate that looks toward the east; and he shall prepare his burnt offering and his peace offerings, as he does on the Sabbath day: then he shall go forth; and after his going forth one shall shut the gate.
13 You shall prepare a lamb a year old without blemish for a burnt offering to Yahweh daily: morning by morning you shall prepare it. 14 You shall prepare a meal offering with it morning by morning, the sixth part of an ephah, and the third part of a hin of oil, to moisten the fine flour; a meal offering to Yahweh continually by a perpetual (*eternal*) ordinance. 15 Thus shall they prepare the lamb, and the meal offering, and the oil, morning by morning, for a continual burnt offering.
19 Then he brought me through the entry, which was at the side of the gate, into the holy rooms for the priests, which looked toward the north: and behold,

there was a place on the hinder part westward. 20 He said to me, This is the place where the priests shall boil the trespass offering and the sin offering, [and] where they shall bake the meal offering; that they not bring them forth into the outer court, to sanctify the people.
21 Then he brought me forth into the outer court, and caused me to pass by the four corners of the court; and behold, in every corner of the court there was a court. 22 In the four corners of the court there were courts enclosed, forty [*cubits*] long (*70 feet, 21 meters*) and thirty broad (*53 feet, 16 meters*): these four in the corners were of one measure. 23 There was a wall around in them, around the four, and boiling places were made under the walls all around. 24 Then he said to me, These are the boiling houses, where the ministers of the house shall boil the sacrifice of the people. (WEB)

After reading all of this, it helps one understand what an incredible privilege we have as the Bride of Christ Jesus. We have free access to Yahweh each and every day. As stated before, the Millennium is the time period of fulfilling all of the promises that God has given to His people, Israel. As some of the people living during this time period are not of the Body of Christ Jesus, but are those who have survived through the Tribulation Period, they do not have daily access to God's throne. Rather, they go through the priesthood of God. However, we who are of the Bride of Christ will have daily access. As His Word explains this in at least three places that I will share next.

Hebrews 4:2-10,16

2 ...we have had good news preached to us, even as they also did, but the word they heard did not profit them, because they were not united by faith with those who heard. 3 For we who have believed do enter into that rest, even as he has said, "As I swore in my wrath, they will not enter into my rest;" although the works were finished from the foundation of the world. 4 For he has said this somewhere about the seventh day, "And God rested on the seventh day from all his works;" 5 and in this place again, "They will not enter into my rest." 6 Since therefore it remains for some to enter it, and they to whom the good news was before preached failed to enter in because of disobedience, 7 he again appoints a certain day, "Today," saying through David so long a time afterward (*just as has been said*), "Today if you will hear his voice, do not harden your hearts." 8 For if Joshua had given them rest, he would not have spoken afterward of another day. 9 There remains therefore a Sabbath rest for the people of God. 10 For he who has entered into his rest has himself also rested from his works, as God did from his. 16 Let us therefore draw near with boldness to the throne of grace, that we may receive mercy, and may find grace for help in time of need. (NHEB)

Ephesians 3:4b-12

4 ...the mystery of Christ; 5 which in other generations was not made known to the children of men, as it has now been revealed to his holy apostles and prophets in the Spirit; 6 that the Gentiles are fellow heirs, and fellow members of the body, and fellow partakers of his promise in Christ Jesus through the Good News, 7 of which I was made a servant, according to the gift of that grace of God which was given me according to

the working of his power. 8 To me, the very least of all saints, was this grace given, to preach to the Gentiles the unsearchable riches of Christ, 9 and to make all men see what is the administration of the mystery which for ages has been hidden in God, who created all things through Jesus Christ; 10 to the intent that now through the assembly the manifold wisdom of God might be made known to the principalities and the powers in the heavenly places, 11 according to the eternal purpose which he purposed in Christ Jesus our Lord; 12 in whom we have boldness and access in confidence through our faith in him. (WEB)

Revelation 7:9-17
9 After these things I looked, and suddenly there was a great multitude, which no one could number, out of every nation and of all tribes, peoples, and languages, standing before the throne and before the Lamb, dressed in white robes, with palm branches in their hands. 10 They shouted with a loud voice, saying, "Salvation be to our God, who sits on the throne, and to the Lamb." 11 All the angels were standing around the throne, the elders, and the four living creatures; and they fell on their faces before the throne, and worshiped God, 12 saying, "Amen. Blessing, glory, wisdom, thanksgiving, honor, power, and might, be to our God forever and ever. Amen."
13 One of the elders answered, saying to me, "These who are arrayed in white robes, who are they, and from where did they come?" 14 So I said to him, "My lord, you know." He said to me, "These are the ones who came out of the great tribulation. They washed their robes, and made them white in the Lamb's blood. 15 Therefore they are before the throne of God, they serve him day and night in his temple. He who sits on

the throne will spread his tabernacle over them. 16 They will hunger no more, neither thirst any more; neither will the sun beat on them, nor any heat; 17 for the Lamb who is in the midst of the throne shepherds them, and leads them to springs of waters of life. And God will wipe away every tear from their eyes." (NHEB)

Inheritance of the land of Israel

On the next page is a map of the land allotment, as I like to have a visual rendition of what I read: Google Image Result for http://www.thebookwurm.com/eze-map.jpg. (n.d.). Www.google.com. Retrieved January 9, 2022, from
<https://images.app.goo.gl/Ax6ASFPYVevpzaCo7>
Used by permission.

You might notice that the measurements I show later in this book are slightly different from what is shown in the picture below. The reason is that the designer of the picture is using the Hebrew Short cubit of 17.5 inches and I am using the Hebrew Long cubit, sometimes called the Hebrew Royal cubit of 20.4 inches. The reason I chose the Hebrew Long cubit is that Ezekiel 43:13 mentions the cubit being a cubit and a handbreadth, being more likely a reference to the Long cubit.

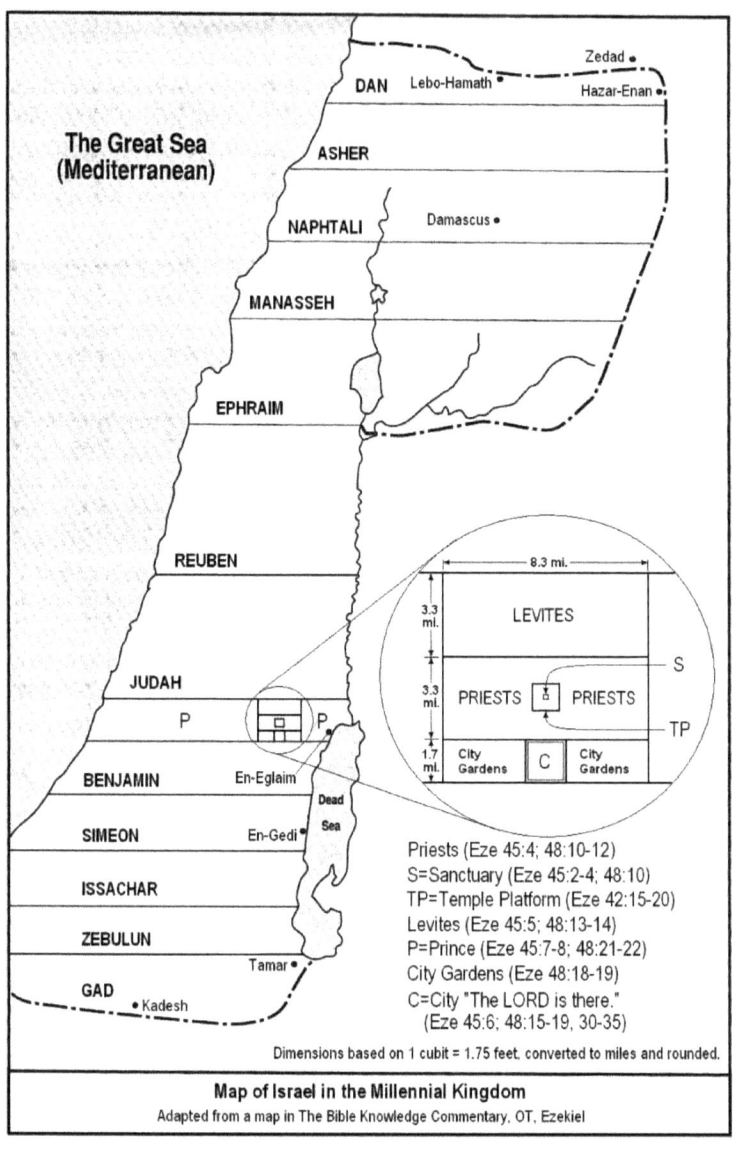

Map of Israel in the Millennial Kingdom
Adapted from a map in The Bible Knowledge Commentary, OT, Ezekiel

Each tribe will be assigned a certain portion of land as their inheritance. They are to offer to the Lord a portion of the entire inherited land, like a tithe. This contribution of land will be set apart for the Temple of

God, which was previously discussed, as well as for the priests and the Levites. It will be an area of land that is 8 miles (13 km) wide and 6.5 miles (11 km) long. You may notice in reading scripture that some show it as 25,000 cubits by 10,000 cubits and other translations show it as 25,000 cubits by 20,000 cubits. According to Ellicott's and the Pulpit Commentary, in the Hebrew language it states it is 25,000 cubits by 10,000 cubits. In the Greek language it is 25,000 cubits by 20,000 cubits. Either way is correct. The reason for this is that the 25,000 x 10,000 cubits is for the sanctuary, then the other 25,000 x 10,000 is for the priests and Levites. It depends upon whether one wants to focus on each part or as the whole. Either way, this entire area will be holy to the Lord. In the 25,000 x 10,000 cubit area an area of 500 cubits x 500 cubits (750 feet, 0.14 miles, 562,500 square feet; 229 meters, 0.229 km, 52,441 square meters) will be specifically for the Holy Place. Eighty-three feet (25 meters) around this area will be for an open space for all to use in common. The Most Holy Place will be limited to only the priests who will be allowed to come before Yahweh to minister to Him. The portion of the city of Jerusalem that belongs to every Israeli, a common area of the city, will be alongside the holy portion. The holy portion is the location of the Temple of God and the place for the priests. This common area will be adjacent to this, consisting of 1.4 miles (2.25 km) wide and 7 miles (11.5 km) long.

In the past, the Levites did not receive any specific parts of the land as an inheritance. During the time of Joshua, in Numbers chapter thirty-five, the Levites were given forty-eight cities throughout all of the land of

Israel. Of these, thirteen were for the priests and six were for cities of refuge. The cities of refuge were a literal place of safety for those guilty of accidentally killing someone. They were to flee to their nearest city of refuge so they would not be killed by family members in response to the death of the person. These cities still belonged to the tribes where the Levitical cities were located, but that is where the Levites were to live, among the people of Israel. Then, during the time of King David in I Chronicles 24, in particular verses 4-5, the priests and Levites were divided into 24 divisions, each to serve a month every two years. Thus, there were houses for them when they served their time in the sanctuary in Jerusalem. However, during the Millennium, the Levites and Priests are given specific land and houses as their own inheritance. Their inherited land will consist of 7 miles (11.5 km) long and 2.8 miles (4.5 km) wide. In verse 5, many translations interpret it as 'towns' to live in. The Hebrew part of that sentence is: לִשְׁכֹּת: עֶשְׂרִים

לְאַחֻזָּה לָהֶם Recall that Hebrew is read right to left. Many commentators speak of the 'towns to live in' rather as 'twenty rooms/chambers.' Some say if one changed a couple of the letters in עֶשְׂרִים to שערים it would read gates/doors, as an entrance into a city. That is how they translate it as town/city. However, others say that one should not change a couple of letters to change the word. I wonder if after the words: 'An area 25,000 cubits long and 10,000 cubits wide will belong to the Levites who serve in the temple' there should be a period instead of a comma and then a new sentence: 'As their possession twenty chambers in the temple.' This would then be in reference to the storage *rooms in the temple needed by the Levites and Priests for all of their supplies, a place to change their clothes, etc., such as what has been mentioned in I Kings 6:5-10 related to the first temple, and the historical document of I Maccabees 4: 38, 57 in reference to the second temple and the future one described in Ezekiel 41:5-11. Then their actual places to live would still be in reference to the 7 miles long by 2.8 miles wide area. This is an interesting aspect of translating from one language to another. As I work as an interpreter I am always dealing with how to best interpret a thought made in one language to a concept in another language so both parties will clearly understand each other. There are many aspects to consider when one is interpreting, not only the words spoken, but also the context in which they are spoken, the cultural understanding of both parties, knowing the actual person who is speaking that includes their personality as well as what makes them who they are and so much more. With God's Word, He is perfect, so there is no misunderstanding on His part or miscues. We are the ones on the receiving end who need to check ourselves. We need to look at the entire context, who He is in His characteristic, the purpose of what is written here and so forth. The Levitical priestly house of Zadok in particular were faithful, acting as watchmen for the whole house of Israel, seeking to preserve the ways of Yahweh. For this reason, a special gift from God will be given to them to inherit the sacred portion of land, bordering the territory of the Levites as explained in Ezekiel 48: 9-12. God never forgets what faithful work you have done for Him.*

There will also be a specific portion of land for the prince as his inheritance. He will be forbidden to take land away from the tribes as he had done in the past for his own use. God will be the one who governs over the prince and rulers. They will not do as they please as they had during historical times for they will be absolutely prohibited from maltreating anyone. What is so reassuring is that we are all the people of God; God is over all of us. When anyone mistreats any one of us, they are actually doing it to God. That person who hurts another will then have to answer to Him, be it the prince all the way down to the youngest child who does a hurtful act under one's own free will decision. The prince's inherited land will border each side of the holy portion of land that will be donated as a tithe to the Lord as well as the city portion of property that is for the entire population. The prince's land will be quite extensive, on the west and east side of the portion of land dedicated to the Lord's service. The prince will use a portion of his land for the weekly and monthly contributions to the Temple as well as for the sin offerings, whole burnt offerings and whatever else will be needed to offer to the Lord for the general population. He will also contribute from his own resources to the pilgrim feasts when everyone will come to celebrate at the Temple before the Lord. Jesus showed what the heart of Elohim is for people in the position of power and authority. Matthew 20: 25-28 says: [25] But Jesus summoned them, and said, "You know that the rulers of the nations lord it over them, and their great ones exercise authority over them. [26] It will not be so among you, but whoever desires to become great among you must be your servant. [27] And whoever desires to be first among you must be your slave, 28 even as the Son of Man did not come to be served, but to serve, and to give his life as a ransom for many." (NHEB) *Therefore, though the prince will have a lot of land, much of it is for the people as a whole.*

Everybody's inheritance will remain within their own family, to their children, grandchildren, and future generations. One may gift some of their property to someone outside the family for up to fifty years, depending on when the Year of Jubilee is in the season of time. At the Year of Jubilee, the property shall revert back to the person who holds the inheritance rights. This shall be for everyone, including the Prince. This is all explained in Leviticus chapter 25. God is concerned about your life and that you have what you need. He does not want anyone to take from a person their rightful inheritance and property, including not being evicted from one's own place. That is never the heart of the Father to have anyone experience this trauma. During the Millennium, this protection shall be ensured. Each family will be given enough property for their future generations to enjoy. Yahweh does not want people scattered around the world away from their rightful possession. During the period of time between the Year of Jubilees if people want to swap properties for the experience of being in another area, they may do so. Also, if one wants to finance their property for payments towards something, they may do so. The amount of money charged will depend upon how many years are left until the Year of Jubilee. However, when the Year of Jubilee hits, the properties will all return to their rightful owners.

Ezekiel chapters 47 to 48 focus specifically on the inherited land in Israel. Even though Dan is not listed as being part of the 144,000 sealed during the Tribulation Period in Revelation 7: 1-8, they are shown here living in the land of Israel. Some of them must have survived through the Tribulation Period. I believe Yahweh will be just as focused on land given to people around the world in regard to what their inherited lots will be as He is here for Israel. However, since His covenant people are in Israel, He focuses specifically on this land. It would have been too extensive in the Bible to delineate every nation's inheritance allotments. Another aspect of the graciousness of God is seen in Ezekiel 27: 21-23. Yahweh says that those who survive through the Tribulation Period and are living within the inherited boundaries of Israel, though are not Israelis by birth, but have their home and children there, will be treated as native born Israelis. They shall inherit their portion of the land where they live. How great the mercy and justice of God is here. Here is a website to help with being able to picture what the inherited land in Israel will be like. (2022). Templemount.org. http://www.templemount.org/LANDIST.JPG from the website: Ezekiel's Temple. (n.d.). Www.templemount.org. Retrieved January 9, 2022, from http://www.templemount.org/ezektmp.html Used by permission. There are also more images available at the bottom of the website page.

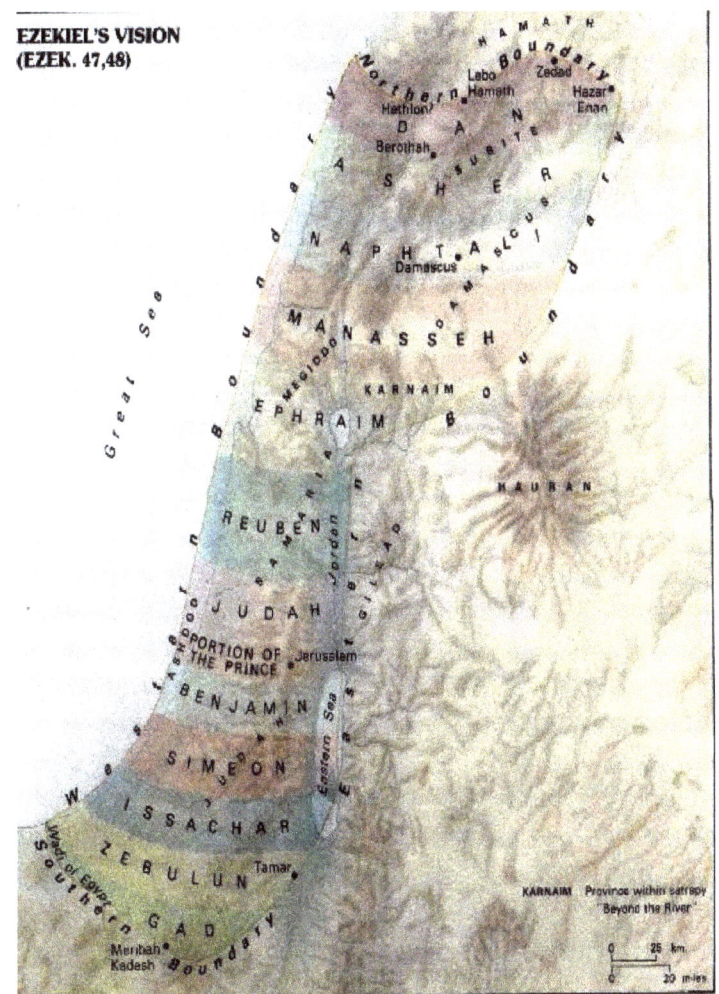

Ezekiel 45: 1 – 8

1 Moreover, when you shall divide by lot the land for inheritance, you shall offer an offering to Yahweh, a holy portion of the land; the length shall be the length of twenty-five thousand [reeds], and the breadth shall be ten thousand (*about 37,500 feet, approximately 7 miles or 11.5 km long and about 30,000 feet, approximately 5.6 miles or 9 km wide*): it shall be holy

in all its border all around. 2 Of this there shall be for the holy place five hundred [in length] by five hundred [*in breadth*] (*about 750 feet square, 229 meters square*), square all around; and fifty cubits (*about 83 feet, 25 meters*) for its suburbs (*open land*) all around. 3 Of this measure you shall measure a length of twenty-five thousand (*about 37,500 feet, app. 7 miles or 11.5 km*), and a breadth of ten thousand (*about 15,000 feet, app. 2.8 miles or 4.5 km*): and in it shall be the sanctuary, which is most holy. 4 It is a holy portion of the land; it shall be for the priests, the ministers of the sanctuary, who come near to minister to Yahweh; and it shall be a place for their houses, and a holy place for the sanctuary. 5 Twenty-five thousand in length, and ten thousand in breadth (*about 37,500 feet, approximately 7 miles or 11.5 km long and about 30,000 feet, approximately 5.6 miles or 9 km wide*), shall be to the Levites, the ministers of the house, for a possession to themselves, [for] twenty rooms (*towns*).

6 You shall appoint the possession of the city five thousand broad (*about 7,500 feet, 1.4 miles or 2.25 km*), and twenty-five thousand long (*about 37,500 feet, app. 7 miles or 11.5 km*), side by side with the offering of the holy portion: it shall be for the whole house of Israel.

7 [Whatever is] for the prince [shall be] on the one side and on the other side of the holy offering and of the possession of the city, in front of the holy offering and in front of the possession of the city, on the west side westward, and on the east side eastward; and in length answerable to one of the portions, from the west border to the east border. 8 In the land it shall be to him for a possession in Israel: and my princes shall

no more oppress my people; but they shall give the land to the house of Israel according to their tribes. (WEB)

Ezekiel 46: 16-18

16 Thus says the Lord (Adonai) Yahweh: If the prince give a gift to any of his sons, it is his inheritance, it shall belong to his sons; it is their possession by inheritance. 17 But if he give of his inheritance a gift to one of his servants, it shall be his to the year of liberty (*Year of Jubilee, every 50th year, Leviticus 25:10*); then it shall return to the prince; but as for his inheritance, it shall be for his sons. 18 Moreover the prince shall not take of the people's inheritance, to thrust them out of their possession; he shall give inheritance to his sons out of his own possession, that my people not be scattered every man from his possession. (WEB)

The Boundaries of the Land

Ezekiel 47: 13-23

13 Thus says the Lord (Adonai) Yahweh: This shall be the border, by which you shall divide the land for inheritance according to the twelve tribes of Israel: Joseph [shall have two] portions. 14 You shall inherit it, one as well as another; for I swore (*uplifted hand, in an oath*) to give it to your fathers: and this land shall fall to you for inheritance.

15 This shall be the border of the land: On the north side, from the great sea, by the way of Hethlon, to the entrance of Zedad; 16 Hamath, Berothah, Sibraim, which is between the border of Damascus and the border of Hamath; Hazer Hatticon, which is by the border of Hauran. 17 The border from the sea, shall be Hazar Enon at the border of Damascus; and on the north northward is the border of Hamath. This is the north side.

18 The east side, between Hauran and Damascus and Gilead, and the land of Israel, shall be the Jordan; from the [north] border to the east sea you shall measure. This is the east side.

19 The south side southward shall be from Tamar as far as the waters of Meriboth Kadesh, to the brook [*of Egypt*], to the great sea. This is the south side southward.

20 The west side shall be the great sea, from the [south] border as far as over against the entrance of Hamath. This is the west side.

21 So you shall divide this land to you according to the tribes of Israel. 22 It shall happen, that you shall divide it by lot for an inheritance to you and to the aliens (*foreigners, not having inherited rights*) who live among

you, who shall father children among you; and they shall be to you as the native-born among the children of Israel; they shall have inheritance (*inherited possession*) with you among the tribes of Israel. 23 It shall happen, that in what tribe the stranger lives, there you shall give him his inheritance, says the Lord (Adonai) Yahweh. (WEB)

The Division of the Land

Ezekiel 48: 1-29
1 Now these are the names of the tribes: From the north end, beside the way of Hethlon to the entrance of Hamath, Hazar Enan (*Village of Fountains*) at the border of Damascus, northward beside Hamath, (and they shall have their sides east [and] west), Dan, one [portion]. 2 By the border of Dan, from the east side to the west side, Asher, one [portion]. 3 By the border of Asher, from the east side even to the west side, Naphtali, one [portion]. 4 By the border of Naphtali, from the east side to the west side, Manasseh, one [portion]. 5 By the border of Manasseh, from the east side to the west side, Ephraim, one [portion]. 6 By the border of Ephraim, from the east side even to the west side, Reuben, one [portion]. 7 By the border of Reuben, from the east side to the west side, Judah, one [portion].
8 By the border of Judah, from the east side to the west side, shall be the offering which you shall offer, twenty-five thousand [reeds] *(about 8 miles, 13 km)* in breadth, and in length as one of the portions, from the east side to the west side: and the sanctuary shall be in its midst. 9 The offering that you shall offer to Yahweh shall be twenty-five thousand [reeds] (*about 8*

miles, 13 km) in length, and ten thousand (*about 3.3 miles, 5.3 km*) in breadth.

The Portion for the Priests

₁₀ For these, even for the priests, shall be the holy offering: toward the north twenty-five thousand (*about 8 miles, 13 km*) [in length], and toward the west ten thousand (*about 3.3 miles, 5.3 km*) in breadth, and toward the east ten thousand (*about 3.3 miles, 5.3 km*) in breadth, and toward the south twenty-five thousand (*about 8 miles, 13 km*) in length: and the sanctuary of Yahweh shall be in its midst. ₁₁ [It shall be] for the priests who are sanctified of the sons of Zadok, who have kept my instruction, who didn't go astray when the children of Israel went astray, as the Levites went astray. ₁₂ It shall be to them an offering from the offering of the land, a thing most holy, by the border of the Levites. ₁₃ Answerable to the border of the priests, the Levites shall have twenty-five thousand (*about 8 miles, 13 km*) in length, and ten thousand (*about 3.3 miles, 5.3 km*) in breadth: all the length shall be twenty-five thousand (*about 8 miles, 13 km*), and the breadth ten thousand (*about 3.3 miles, 5.3 km*). ₁₄ They shall sell none of it, nor exchange it, nor shall the first fruits of the land be alienated; for it is holy to Yahweh.

₁₅ The five thousand (*1.6 miles, 2.7 km*) that are left in the breadth, in front of the twenty-five thousand (*about 8 miles, 13 km*), shall be for common (*general, ordinary, not sacred*) use, for the city, for dwelling and for suburbs (*pastureland, open land*); and the city shall be in its midst. ₁₆ These shall be its measures: the north side four thousand and five hundred (*1.5 miles,*

2.4 km), and the south side four thousand and five hundred (*1.5 miles, 2.4 km*), and on the east side four thousand and five hundred (*1.5 miles, 2.4 km*), and the west side four thousand and five hundred (*1.5 miles, 2.4 km*). 17 The city shall have suburbs (*pastureland, open land*): toward the north two hundred fifty *(440 feet, 135 meters)*, and toward the south two hundred fifty (*440 feet, 135 meters*), and toward the east two hundred fifty (*440 feet, 135 meters*), and toward the west two hundred fifty (*440 feet, 135 meters*). 18 The remainder in the length, answerable to the holy offering, shall be ten thousand (*about 3.3 miles, 5.3 km*) eastward, and ten thousand (*about 3.3 miles, 5.3 km*) westward; and it shall be answerable to the holy offering; and its increase (*farmland, crop land*) shall be for food to those who labor in the city. 19 Those who labor in the city, out of all the tribes of Israel, shall cultivate it. 20 All the offering shall be twenty-five thousand by twenty-five thousand (*about 8 miles, 13 km wide and long*): you shall offer the holy offering foursquare, with the possession of the city.

The Portion for the Prince

21 The residue shall be for the prince, on the one side and on the other of the holy offering and of the possession of the city; in front of the twenty-five thousand (*about 8 miles, 13 km*) of the offering toward the east border, and westward in front of the twenty-five thousand (*about 8 miles, 13 km*) toward the west border, answerable to the portions, it shall be for the prince: and the holy offering and the sanctuary of the house shall be in its midst. 22 Moreover from the possession of the Levites, and from the possession of

the city, being in the midst of that which is the prince's, between the border of Judah and the border of Benjamin, it shall be for the prince.

The Portion for Remaining Tribes

23 As for the rest of the tribes: from the east side to the west side, Benjamin, one [portion]. 24 By the border of Benjamin, from the east side to the west side, Simeon, one [portion]. 25 By the border of Simeon, from the east side to the west side, Issachar, one [portion]. 26 By the border of Issachar, from the east side to the west side, Zebulun, one [portion]. 27 By the border of Zebulun, from the east side to the west side, Gad, one [portion]. 28 By the border of Gad, at the south side southward, the border shall be even from Tamar (*land of palm trees*) to the waters of Meribath Kadesh, to the brook (*dry stream bed except when it rains*) [of Egypt], to the great sea. 29 This is the land which you shall divide by lot to the tribes of Israel for inheritance, and these are their several portions, says the Lord (Adonai) Yahweh. (WEB)

The Gates of the New City

Ezekiel 48: 30-35
30 These are the exits of the city: On the north side four thousand and five hundred [reeds] (*1.5 miles, 2.4 km*) by measure; 31 and the gates of the city shall be after the names of the tribes of Israel, three gates northward: the gate of Reuben, one; the gate of Judah, one; the gate of Levi, one. 32 At the east side four thousand and five hundred [reeds] (*1.5 miles, 2.4 km*), and three gates: even the gate of Joseph, one; the

gate of Benjamin, one; the gate of Dan, one. ₃₃ At the south side four thousand and five hundred [reeds] (*1.5 miles, 2.4 km*) by measure, and three gates: the gate of Simeon, one; the gate of Issachar, one; the gate of Zebulun, one. ₃₄ At the west side four thousand and five hundred [reeds] (*1.5 miles, 2.4 km*), with their three gates: the gate of Gad, one; the gate of Asher, one; the gate of Naphtali, one. ₃₅ It shall be eighteen thousand [reeds] (*6 miles, 9.5 km*) around: and the name of the city from that day shall be, Yahweh is there. (WEB)

Yahweh will be moved with compassion toward the desert land and uninhabited land of Zion due to its harsh environment, changing it into a life-giving area of beauty. From what I know of deserts, there are some deserts that seem to be void of life, with the exception of the hardiest animals and insects. Locations like this include areas of land that only receive less than two inches of rain per year, such as the Atacama in Chile. The land is primarily sand and rocks with only the toughest of plants surviving as well as some well adapted mammals, reptiles, birds, and insects. Then there are other deserts, like the Namib Desert in Southwestern Africa, Sonoran Desert, and Chihuahuan Desert in southwest US along with northern Mexico, being some of the most biodiverse deserts in the world, full of life and beauty. In the beginning, Elohim created the genetic material within living entities to be able to adapt to numerous different climates and issues that would arise. He is incredible in His creativity and design. During the Millennium, the desert land of Israel will flourish and bloom. Even saffron will flourish there. Saffron is an expensive spice from the Middle East and

Mediterranean area used for its complex flavor with a hint of sweetness and health factors, being high in antioxidants. If you may recall, the living water that pours forth from the Temple of God will pour down into the desert areas filling the dry, seasonal wadis. These wadis will no longer be dry and intermittently filled with water, rather they will be full all year-round. In the southwest US we call these intermittently dry streambeds 'washes,' which are dry most of the year. However, they can dangerously fill up to become a rushing river during the monsoon rains. For video examples of this and more information, go to For More Study, 7. During the Millennium, what used to be a dry, uninhabited land in Israel will become like the land of Eden. It will be a garden-like land, which is currently found on Mt. Carmel, Israel. It will also look like the lush plains of Sharon that surround Mt. Carmel. The riverbeds will no longer be dangerous, but life-giving. Water will spring up in the wilderness turning the hot, parched land into aromatic ponds that will grow semi-aquatic plants, such as leeks, sweet calamus and papyrus. It will become a place of beauty.

There will be a highway that goes through this area, which leads to Jerusalem. It will be called the Way of Holiness. It will only be for those who live in a godly manner of life. God is a life giver and His ways propagate life. Some people twist this thought, thinking their own ways apart from God will provide an enjoyable life, but in the end will only bring forth death, to themselves and others. Think back to Adam and Eve. They thought taking the fruit of the tree would bring them everything they wanted. Instead, it brought forth death, pain, and suffering for innumerable generations. The impure will not be allowed to travel on this road. In fact, those who despise wisdom are quarrelsome, and mock when being found guilty will not even be allowed to wander onto it. Only the redeemed by the Kinsman-Redeemer (Yeshua HaMashiach: Jesus our Messiah) and those Yahweh has ransomed from exile, restoring them to Himself shall be on this road. The Torah, God's Law and divine instruction will go forth from this road unto all the nations. The execution of justice will go forth from this road and cases will be decided. Righteousness in governance will spread across the globe speedily. Those who are in need of rescue, deliverance, and safety will receive it from the Lord. Those in the farthest region of the globe will look for Yahweh expectantly waiting for His strong arm of morality and righteousness to execute justice, bringing light to all the nations. As Proverbs 29: 2 and 26 say: [2] When the righteous thrive, the people rejoice; but when the wicked rule, the people groan. [26] Many seek the ruler's favor, but a man's justice comes from Yahweh. (WEB) *Therefore, strengthen your feeble hands, and steady yourself. Speak to your fearful heart and mind to be courageous, knowing that you have no reason to be in dread of Elohim as He has already victoriously saved you. People walking to Zion will not encounter any danger the entire way. Even venomous snakes, lions, or any other dangerous animals will not be allowed to inhabit the area around the road. This is reiterated in* Isaiah 11:6-9 [6] The wolf will live with the lamb, and the leopard will lie down with the young goat; The calf and the young lion will graze together; and a little child will lead them. [7] The cow and the bear will graze. Their young ones will lie down together. The lion will eat straw like the ox. [8] The nursing child will play near a cobra's hole, and the weaned child will put his hand on the viper's den. 9 They will not hurt nor destroy in all my holy mountain; for the earth will be full of the knowledge of the LORD, as the waters cover the sea. (NHEB) *Any grief and groaning will flee away from each person as they walk along the road. The eyes of the blind will be opened and the ears of the deaf will be unstopped. The lame will leap like a deer and the mute will begin to shout for joy. Gladness and joy will spring up from within the innermost parts of each person. The entire road to Zion will be surrounded by the sounds of thankful rejoicing and the playing of a large variety of instruments from around the world. Singing praises unto Yahweh will overflow from this road throughout the earth.*

Isaiah 35: 1-10
1 The wilderness (*uninhabited land*) and the dry land will be glad. The desert will rejoice and blossom like a rose (*meadow saffron*).
2 It will blossom abundantly, and rejoice even with joy and singing. Lebanon's glory (*abundance*) Lebanon will be given to it, the excellence of Carmel and Sharon. They will see Yahweh's glory, the excellence of our God (Elohim).
3 Strengthen the weak hands, and make firm the feeble knees.
4 Tell those who have a fearful heart, "Be strong. Don't be afraid. Behold, your God (Elohim) will come with vengeance, God's (Elohim's) retribution. He will come and save you.
5 Then the eyes of the blind will be opened, and the ears of the deaf will be unstopped.
6 Then the lame man will leap like a deer, and the

tongue of the mute will sing; for waters will break out in the wilderness, and streams in the desert.

7 The burning sand will become a pool, and the thirsty ground springs of water. Grass with reeds and rushes will be in the habitation of jackals (*venomous snakes*), where they lay.

8 A highway will be there, a road, and it will be called The Holy Way. The unclean shall not pass over it, but it will be for those who walk in the Way. Wicked fools will not go there.

9 No lion will be there, nor will any ravenous animal go up on it. They will not be found there; but the redeemed will walk there.

10 Then Yahweh's ransomed ones will return, and come with singing to Zion; and everlasting joy will be on their heads. They will obtain gladness and joy, and sorrow and sighing will flee away." (WEB)

Isaiah 51: 3-5

3 For Yahweh has comforted Zion; he has comforted all her waste places, and has made her wilderness like Eden, and her desert like the garden of Yahweh; joy and gladness shall be found therein, thanksgiving, and the voice of melody.

4 "Attend to me, my people; and give ear to me, my nation: for a law shall go forth from me, and I will establish my justice for a light of the peoples.

5 My righteousness is near, my salvation is gone forth, and my arms shall judge the peoples; the islands shall wait for me, and on my arm shall they trust. (WEB)

End of the Thousand Years and Judgment of Satan

In Revelation 20:2 ₂ He seized the dragon, the old serpent, which is the devil and Satan, who deceives the whole inhabited earth, and bound him for a thousand years. (WEB) *The name 'devil' implies one who slanders, falsely accuses, and severs relationships through condemnation. This work of his will not be operational until the end of the thousand-year period.*

After the thousand years are completed, Satan will be set free to again accomplish his deception for a micro interval of time. During this duration of testing, people will be given the choice between serving Yahweh or believing the deception like Adam and Eve did. Satan will go out to all regions of the earth, to the groups of people joined together with similar cultural foundations and belief systems to deceptively question the true intentions and character of Elohim. He will also appeal to the desire to evaluate things as supposedly right in one's own eyes. The strategy he will employ would make it appear that if they follow his ways they will not miss out on something that should be supposedly rightfully theirs. If they were to ignore him and his ways, they would lose out on what is theirs to take. As I John 2: 15-17 says: ₁₅ Don't love the world, neither the things that are in the world. If anyone loves the world, the Father's love isn't in him. ₁₆ For all that is in the world, the lust of the flesh, the lust of the eyes, and the pride of life, isn't the Father's, but is the world's. ₁₇ The world is passing away with its lusts, but he who does God's will remains forever. (WEB) *God allows this deception to let people freely pick sides, if they are for or against Yahweh. Their decision will affect their placement for eternity. The area of the earth that will be a key region of deception will be in Gog and Magog. Ezekiel chapter 38, in particular verses 1-6 speak the most about this area. Gog is a remote region in the northern part of the land of Magog. It comprises Meshek, who was the son of Japheth, Genesis 10:2, a location near Armenia and Tubal, an area around Turkey. An innumerable army of humanity will assemble to come against the city of God. God will wait until the entirety of armed forces coming from all areas of the earth arrive at the doorstep of Yahweh's beloved city, surrounding it. Therefore, they will all be in one location. They will all gather together in a cramped place, not one of them will be missing or left behind. Since they will have sinned against Yahweh, they will blindly come to surround the City of God, like the blind leading the blind as addressed in Matthew 15:14. Then Yahweh will send fire down from heaven and utterly consume them, leaving absolutely nothing left of them. Their silver and gold will not be able to deliver them on the day of Yahweh's fury. All of the presumptuous and enemies of God will be turned to chaff, blown away into nothingness. It will be as if they were never there. Not a root or a branch will be left to them. The devil, who falsely accuses others, severing relationships between people and bringing in deception will be apprehended and thrown into the lake of burning sulfur, where the beast and false prophet already have been thrown. They will all be tormented with grievous pains of mind and body day and night for eternity. All those who followed Satan and his ways will suffer the same fate. They will cry out from mental and physical pain. Their mind and understanding will remain intact. They will howl from their spirit being continually crushed. Their names will be abandoned as a curse.*

During the Millennium, it will not yet be perfect, meaning everyone living without sin, as it will still be filled with humans who possess the human nature passed down from Adam to them. Yes, those of the First Resurrection will be alive and reigning over the people living during this time. We will no longer be under the effects of the Adamic nature, having been made new in Christ Jesus. However, those living during this time, having made it through the Tribulation Period or born during the Millennium, will still have the free-will to choose Yahweh or choose their own ways. This will be made very evident when Satan is set free for a microcosm of time at the end of the Millennium. Often people think that they have been given free liberty to do what is evil in God's sight as His patience is exceedingly great. His grace often spans multiple human generations. The first few generations will appear to have gotten by with their evil activities scot-free. These activities often negatively affect a sizable number of people. However, when it is done by nations, these effects will traumatize people even outside of its sphere of control. Unknowingly, each generation is piling up judgment into the unseen receptacle until it comes to a breaking point and is poured out.

Piling up judgment can be likened to a generational hoarder. Each piece is added individually. At first, it doesn't amount to much and is often overlooked. Then a few generations down the line, living on the same property, the piles start to appear filling the garage and then some rooms, but nobody outside notices. The rooms are just closed off one by one. Then years down the road, small, manageable piles begin to appear in the backyard, consequently being stashed in a shed and then two. Yet, it is still for the most part hidden away from view. Give it a number of additional years and the piles from the backyard begin to pour into the front yard in small, manageable piles. This is usually when the neighborhood begins to notice and talk. Quite a number of years later the whole yard is filled with junk, leaving only a pathway to get to the door. It is now that the town is called in to deal with this nuisance property and possibly rescue the large number of animals living uncontrollably outside and uncared for inside the house. This is when judgment comes down. There was the hope that one of those generations would look around and want to make a change, cleaning up the growing mess. However, one generation after another came to believe this manner of life was an accepted practice; it was who they had become. On top of this, it had grown too hard to change who they had been known for generationally. It became part of their identity.

God really does not want to destroy a person in judgment as He has individually made each one of us with amazing potential. It is His innate desire that each one of us walks into the potential built into us. He desires that one person in the generational line will wake up and unearth that incredible potential, breaking free from the chains and filth surrounding them. However, there comes a point like the generational hoarder when judgment finally comes handed down. So, it will be at the end of the Millennium.

Isaiah chapter sixty-five speaks very well to this in my estimation. The people God reaches out to the most are often those who spurn Him to the face the bulk of time. A number of these people will take Him for granted and often believe that since their ancestors served God they are automatically grandfathered into this blessing as well; therefore, there are no worries. They will apostatize from the Lord, ignoring His ways and attributes. They will stubbornly live out their own lives pursuing their own plans, purposes, inventions, and imaginations. They will turn to fortune, fate, and karma as what determines a person's lot in life. They will cease to care for Yahweh, turning away from listening to Him and His warnings, instead doing what is ethically wrong. They will say that they are serving Yahweh, while secretly serving other gods. They will convince others in their debates and conversations that what God sees as good is actually evil and what God sees as evil is actually good. They will pull the wool over people's eyes telling them that they just do not understand the deep ways and truths of God. They will tell other people they are much holier and more devout than others and what they assert is correct. However, God sees what is truly happening in their heart and will not remain silent forever. In a preordained time, God will pay them back for their misdeeds and perversion. He will wait for the opportune time in that He does not and will not destroy the righteous with the wicked. Also, He knows when there is still potential for goodness to come forth from a person. It is when that potential has been exhausted and the time has come to an end that judgment comes. He will separate the righteous from the wicked first before His judgment is handed down. In the fire of Yahweh's passionate anger, the totality of earth will be devoured with fire, bringing a sudden annihilation of all who reside on the earth. The Day of the Lord will arrive unexpectedly for the wicked. For the righteous, they will be expectantly awaiting His act of bringing an end to all things and making everything new. As Yahweh has promised in His Word, the new Heaven and earth will be a fresh beginning, superior to what preceded it. Righteousness will be permanently established. When the nations come at the end of the Millennium to surround Yahweh's beloved city, those who have chosen Yahweh will be inside of His city. They will be feasting, conducting their lives influenced by the Holy Spirit, but the enemies of God will be put to shame outside of the camp. The servants of God will sing out in joy and exultation when Yahweh strikes His enemies dead in one sweep of His hand. They will go out and leap like well-fed calves. They will trample the ashes of the ungodly under their feet. Yahweh of the angelic armies will accomplish this.

At this point in time, being the end of the Millennium with each person alive having made their choice for eternity, Heaven and earth will be done away with making way for the completely new one to be created. Yahweh will gather together the totality of everything, mankind, beasts of the earth, birds, insects, sea creatures as well as everything that caused a stumbling block for humans. All that is seen will vanish like smoke that is blown away in the wind. The heavens will disappear with a loud, rushing noise. The basic components of the orderly arrangement of the universe, the material elements will have all their elemental bonds dissolved and rendered void by a great heat.

The earth and everything created will be completely burned up, no longer to be found anywhere. Not even one element or quark will be left in existence. Earth will be used up completely, like an old garment. Those who are alive and remain on earth will all physically die, both the young and old alike. Yahweh's righteousness and those who belong to Yahweh shall remain forever, even though their earthly bodies are destroyed. They will be given new, spiritual bodies that are designed for eternity.

Isaiah 65: 1-16
1 "I am inquired of by those who didn't ask; I am found by those who didn't seek me: I said, See me, see me, to a nation that was not called by my name.
2 I have spread out my hands all the day to a rebellious people, who walk in a way that is not good, after their own thoughts;
3 a people who provoke me to my face continually, sacrificing in gardens, and burning incense on bricks;
4 who sit among the graves, and lodge in the secret places; who eat pig's flesh, and broth of abominable things is in their vessels;
5 who say, Stand by yourself, don't come near to me, for I am holier than you. These are a smoke in my nose, a fire that burns all the day.
6 "Behold, it is written before me: I will not keep silence, but will recompense, yes, I will recompense into their bosom,
7 your own iniquities, and the iniquities of your fathers together," says Yahweh, "who have burned incense on the mountains, and blasphemed me on the hills; therefore will I first measure their work into their bosom."

₈ Thus says Yahweh, "As the new wine is found in the cluster, and one says, 'Don't destroy it, for a blessing is in it:' so will I do for my servants' sake, that I may not destroy them all.

₉ I will bring forth a seed out of Jacob, and out of Judah an inheritor of my mountains; and my chosen shall inherit it, and my servants shall dwell there.

₁₀ Sharon shall be a fold of flocks, and the valley of Achor a place for herds to lie down in, for my people who have sought me.

₁₁ "But you who forsake Yahweh, who forget my holy mountain, who prepare a table for Fortune, and who fill up mixed wine to Destiny;

₁₂ I will destine you to the sword, and you shall all bow down to the slaughter; because when I called, you did not answer; when I spoke, you did not hear; but you did that which was evil in my eyes, and chose that in which I didn't delight."

₁₃ Therefore thus says the Lord (Adonai) Yahweh, "Behold, my servants shall eat, but you shall be hungry; behold, my servants shall drink, but you shall be thirsty; behold, my servants shall rejoice, but you shall be disappointed;

₁₄ behold, my servants shall sing for joy of heart, but you shall cry for sorrow of heart, and shall wail for anguish of spirit.

₁₅ You shall leave your name for a curse to my chosen; and the Lord (Adonai) Yahweh will kill you; and he will call his servants by another name:

₁₆ so that he who blesses himself in the earth shall bless himself in the God (Elohim) of truth; and he who swears in the earth shall swear by the God (Elohim) of truth; because the former troubles are forgotten, and because they are hidden from my eyes. (WEB)

Revelation 20: 7-10

7 And after the thousand years, Satan will be released from his prison, 8 and he will come out to deceive the nations which are in the four corners of the earth, Gog and Magog, to gather them together to the war; the number of whom is as the sand of the sea. 9 They went up over the breadth of the earth, and surrounded the camp of the saints, and the beloved city. Fire came down out of heaven from God, and devoured them. 10 The devil who deceived them was thrown into the lake of fire and sulfur, where the beast and the false prophet are also. They will be tormented day and night forever and ever. (WEB)

Zephaniah 1: 17-18

17 I will bring distress on men, that they will walk like blind men, because they have sinned against Yahweh, and their blood will be poured out like dust, and their flesh like dung.
18 Neither their silver nor their gold will be able to deliver them in the day of Yahweh's wrath, but the whole land will be devoured by the fire of his jealousy; for he will make an end, yes, a terrible end, of all those who dwell in the land. (WEB)

Malachi 4: 1-3

1 "For, behold, the day comes, it burns as a furnace; and all the proud, and all who work wickedness, will be stubble; and the day that comes will burn them up," says Yahweh of Armies (*Angelic Armies*), "that it shall leave them neither root nor branch. 2 But to you who fear my name shall the sun of righteousness arise with healing in its wings. You will go out, and leap like calves of the stall. 3 You shall tread down the wicked; for they will be ashes under the soles of your feet in

the day that I make," says Yahweh of Armies (*Angelic Armies*). (WEB)

Zephaniah 1: 2-3
2 I will utterly sweep away everything off of the surface of the earth, says Yahweh.
3 I will sweep away man and animal. I will sweep away the birds of the sky, the fish of the sea, and the heaps of rubble with the wicked. I will cut off man from the surface of the earth, says Yahweh. (WEB)

Isaiah 51: 6-8
6 Lift up your eyes to the heavens, and look on the earth beneath; for the heavens shall vanish away like smoke, and the earth shall wax old like a garment; and those who dwell therein shall die in the same way: but my salvation shall be forever, and my righteousness shall not be abolished.
7 "Listen to me, you who know righteousness, the people in whose heart is my law (*Torah, God's Law, Divine Instruction*); don't fear the reproach of men, neither be dismayed at their insults.
8 For the moth shall eat them up like a garment, and the worm shall eat them like wool; but my righteousness shall be forever, and my salvation to all generations." (WEB)

II Peter 3:7, 10-13
7 But the heavens that now are, and the earth, by the same word have been stored up for fire, being reserved against the day of judgment and destruction of ungodly men. 10 But the day of the Lord will come as a thief in the night; in which the heavens will pass away with a great noise, and the elements will be dissolved with fervent heat, and the earth and the

works that are in it will be burned up.

11 Therefore since all these things will be destroyed like this, what kind of people ought you to be in holy living and godliness, 12 looking for and earnestly desiring the coming of the day of God, which will cause the burning heavens to be dissolved, and the elements will melt with fervent heat? 13 But, according to his promise, we look for new heavens and a new earth, in which righteousness dwells. (WEB)

The Judgment of the Dead

As every created thing of the old creation is now completely incinerated and absolutely everything is put under the rulership of Yeshua HaMashiach, death no longer has its say. It has been destroyed along with all the previous creation; fully abolished and having no effect. The final enemy, death, has now been put under Elohim's feet and its power altogether shattered. All that is left in existence are the eternal souls/spirits of all humanity, the demons/angels as they are also eternal, along with Elohim, the Godhead. In the beginning, as the Word of God says, Jesus created everything. It also says Elohim created everything. The Trinity worked together in unity. Now Jesus entrusts the Kingdom to God the Father as Yeshua HaMashiach is now over everything. All former dominions, including earthly, demonic, of any origin outside of God's hands, including all of their deceptions are rendered inoperable and have absolutely no effect on anyone or anything. It is the fulfillment of Psalm 110:1: [1] Yahweh says to my Lord (*Adon*), "Sit at my right hand, until I make your enemies your footstool for your feet." (WEB)

I Corinthians 15: 24-28
[24] Then the end comes, when he will deliver up the Kingdom to God, even the Father; when he will have abolished all rule and all authority and power. [25] For he must reign until he has put all his enemies under his feet. [26] The last enemy that will be abolished is death. [27] For, "He put all things in subjection under his feet." But when he says, "All things are put in subjection," it is evident that he is excepted who subjected all things to him. [28] When all things have been subjected to him, then the Son will also himself

be subjected to him who subjected all things to him, that God may be all in all. (WEB)

Heaven and earth having now vanished, thrones are set up and the brilliant white throne of God, the Ancient of Days, arrives. His clothing is white as snow and the hair of His head is like pure white wool. His throne is flaming with fire and a river of fire pours forth from His presence. The cherubim with wheels within wheels who accompany God's throne are all ablaze. For more information on how this all looks see Ezekiel chapter one. There are thousands upon thousands attending Him. There are also myriads upon myriads, which is at least 10,000 x 10,000, 10^8 or hundred million plus, standing before Him. People might come forth as groups associated with different ages to be judged. As Elohim sits upon His throne, the last judgment begins.

Every place where the dead were before the past creation was eternally erased from existence, be it from the past sea, from Hades or any other prior location will now all be released to stand before the Great White Throne of God for judgment. It doesn't matter if they were great or insignificant during their lifetime, they will all stand together in front of Elohim's throne for judgment. Small books will be opened. One translation of this book could be understood as bills of divorcement, the ending of any and all covenantal vows between the two parties. Then a different small book is brought forward and it is opened. This last small book brought forward is the Book of Eternal Life. The dead are judged as being guilty or innocent according to their actions recorded in these books. Anyone whose name is not found to be written in the Book of Eternal Life is found to be guilty. The determination of guilt means that they are spiritually dead, being separated from the life of God. There is nothing here that talks about if one's good works outweigh one's bad works for the determination of guilt or innocence. The only determining factor is if your name is written in the Book of Eternal Life, having the life of God through Christ Jesus. God, being so good and not wanting anyone to be judged as guilty, doesn't hide anything from anyone. If you want to presently know if you will be judged as innocent or guilty, it is already laid out beforehand in His Word, the Bible, so there is no excuse of ignorance. Those in the Old Testament looked forward through the promises of God for the awaited Messiah. The first promise was given in Genesis 3:15, 21, 4:3-4 15 I will put enmity between you and the woman, and between your offspring and her offspring. He will bruise your head, and you will bruise his heel." 21 Yahweh God (Elohim) made coats of skins for Adam and for his wife, and clothed them. 3 As time passed, it happened that Cain brought an offering to Yahweh from the fruit of the ground. 4 Abel also brought some of the firstborn of his flock and of its fat. Yahweh respected Abel and his offering. (WEB) *Abel was looking unto the Lamb of God promised by Elohim. They knew from the very beginning that God had a plan of redemption. You can see this scarlet thread woven throughout the entire Bible. This is a whole other study, which I would highly recommend you undertake as you read the Bible cover to cover. At the conclusion of the judgment, death and Hades are cast into the Lake of Fire. Then anyone whose name is not found to be written in the Book of Eternal Life is also thrown into the Lake of Fire. This is the second death, complete separation from God for eternity.*

The Ancient of Days will have already pronounced judgment in favor of each and every one of the holy people who have eternal life with the Most High at the onset of the Millennial Kingdom as shown in Revelation 20:4-6 and I Corinthians 15: 20-28. Then those who are alive during the Millennial, having not yet physically died, it appears there will be a dividing of the people. Those who chose God and His ways will be in the City of God with Him and those against Him will be outside of the City of God to attack it as previously described in chapter 'End of the Thousand Years and Judgment of Satan.' It reminds me of when God dealt with the Israelites time and again as they opposed Moses, the leader Yahweh set up in their midst. One of these instances is when judgment was pronounced by God on the Levitical family of Korah and those who followed them versus Moses in Numbers chapter 16. God caused the earth to open up and swallow the families of Korah, Dathan and Abiram alive followed by the fire of God consuming the two hundred fifty other men who were acting in the role of priests, which they were not. At this point, being the end of the Millennial period, the time will have come that the people of God possess the kingdom promised to them. He will hand over the sovereignty, power, and greatness of all the kingdoms that were under heaven to the holy people of the Most High God. His kingdom will be an everlasting kingdom with all those in power worshipping and fully obeying Him.

Revelation 20: 11-15

[11] I saw a great white throne, and him who sat on it, from whose face the earth and the heaven fled away. There was found no place for them. [12] I saw the dead,

the great and the small, standing before the throne, and they opened books. Another book was opened, which is the book of life (*eternal life*). The dead were judged out of the things which were written in the books, according to their works. 13 The sea gave up the dead who were in it. Death and Hades gave up the dead who were in them. They were judged, each one according to his works. 14 Death and Hades were thrown into the lake of fire. This is the second death, the lake of fire. 15 If anyone was not found written in the book of life (*eternal life*), he was cast into the lake of fire. (WEB)

Daniel 7: 9-10, 13-14, 22, 27
9 I saw until thrones were placed, and one who was ancient of days sat: his clothing was white as snow, and the hair of his head like pure wool; his throne was fiery flames, [and] its wheels burning fire.
10 A fiery stream issued and came forth from before him: thousands of thousands ministered to him, and ten thousand times ten thousand stood before him: the judgment was set, and the books were opened. 13 I saw in the night visions, and behold, there came with the clouds of the sky one like a son of man, and he came even to the Ancient of Days, and they brought him near before him.
14 There was given him dominion, and glory, and a kingdom, that all the peoples, nations, and languages should serve him: his dominion is an everlasting dominion, which shall not pass away, and his kingdom that which shall not be destroyed. 22 ...the Ancient of Days came, and judgment was given to the saints of the Most High, and the time came that the saints possessed the kingdom. 27 The kingdom and

the dominion, and the greatness of the kingdoms under the whole sky, shall be given to the people of the saints of the Most High: his kingdom is an everlasting kingdom, and all dominions shall serve and obey him. (WEB)

Entering Eternity

A New Heaven and a New Earth

Elohim will promptly and completely create a new heavens and earth, superior to what was before it as righteousness will be permanently established in the totality of it. Elohim is making all things new, superior to what was previously in existence. Jesus promises that all of these words are trustworthy and genuine. In fact, in His sight all of this is already done and in effect as He lives outside of our finiteness in our present world, seeing all from the beginning to the end and beyond. II Peter chapter three speaks to this, especially verses seven and ten to thirteen. The word 'create' in Isaiah 65:17 is the same word that was used in Genesis 1:1: בָּרָא to divinely shape or create. All that happened prior to this new creation will not be brought back to mind or mentioned. Elohim will completely remove and erase every kind of mental and physical tear from prior crying. There will no longer be physical or spiritual death, mourning, grief, emotionally packed wailing, or suffering. The sound of weeping or cries of distress will never be heard again. For the previous old order of things will be fully gone. In the reality of God, all that He has said is truly already completed, without question. As He has promised in His Word, His people will build houses and not be removed from them. They will plant gardens, vineyards and orchards and enjoy the fruit of their labors. They will enjoy the work of their hands in everything they wish to do. All of this will be done in the new heavens and the new earth.

For us, living in a time constrained world, our ability to see much outside of our own life experience can be challenging. It is similar to a person being stopped at a train track crossing where the current location of the *train track is at a curve, running through a deep forest. As we watch the train come towards us, the forest is not as thick as it is on the other side; thus, we can see further down the tracks and more of the train as it comes towards us. However, as we watch where the train proceeds, it quickly disappears around the curve into the thick woods, out of sight. We watch every train car pass by before us as we wait, pondering where the end of the train will be so we may cross over the tracks to continue to the other side. God, however, is like one who is flying a drone, high above the train tracks and the road intersecting it. He can see the whole train as well as far beyond it in all directions, where it came from, where it is going, its destination and much more. As He is the Alpha, unoriginated originator of all life and the Omega, having absolute limitless ability to meet all the needs of a limited people as well as being the Beginning, Chief, at the same time the End, consummation and aim of all life. All that He says and each and every one of His promises are truly fulfilled.*

The new creation will return to how it was intended when He first created everything, including the earth and mankind. His desire is to be in an intimate relationship with us, to walk and talk with us, being in harmonious fellowship together. Before a person speaks out to Yahweh, He will answer them. Yahweh will intimately listen to everything a person says. Even before He created all of the angels and mankind, along with all of the original creation, He had intimate fellowship with Himself as the triune God. Having an intimate relationship with others is the core of who He is as well as desiring to lavishly adore and bless those whom He loves. All of mankind living in the new creation will come before Yahweh, in His presence, worshipping Him and experiencing an unending closeness with Elohim. We will be inseparable.

The entirety of the new earth will be a reflection of how it was first created to be before the fall of mankind. The time period between the fall of Adam and Eve and the new heavens and new earth are comparable to a parenthesis of time. When mankind fell into sin, it led to a pause in Elohim's perfect intentions for the original creation. It did not happen as a surprise to Elohim. He knew it would happen when He first created the first heavens and the first earth. However, out of love, He still created it all and worked His grace through it all. Now that the end of the parenthesis has happened, we pick up with how He intended it to be in the beginning. There will no longer be any sin or effects from sin in everything, except the designated prison of the Lake of Fire. That will be eternally barricaded off from everything, even from His presence of love and grace. There will no longer be any predation as each animal will only eat vegetation. There will no longer be any harm or ruination happening. What is intriguing to me is that there are no longer any *large bodies of water, such as seas or large lakes*. Rather, as is mentioned in Revelation 21:6, there will be springs of water. Could this mean that there will not be large bodies of water separating people? Will God bring the earth back to a similar way He created it in the beginning, with one enormous land mass and one ocean? Therefore, might there still be whales to watch and the peaceful enjoyment of the beaches? We shall find out as we watch Him create the New Earth and then have time to explore it throughout eternity. The *creativeness of God is infinite. There will be so much to probe into and research for enjoyment. Revelation 22:1 also speaks of rivers. I am curious to find out if there will be mists that arise up from the earth and water the whole surface of the ground as was mentioned in Genesis 2:6. I guess in time we will also find out if there will be rising mists or not. Just as this new heavens and new earth will remain continually, without end, so shall the trueness of who each of us are. We will remain active and alive forever in Christ Jesus. This is so exciting to me and I am eager to find out what all of this will look like in eternity. This will be our forever home!*

I am unsure if the new universe will be under the constraints of time, such as what we have experienced in our present lifetime relative to the Theory of Relativity. I see in the creation of the first universe that time was created. However, the tracking of time, such as the phases of the moon, the sun and the tracking of the constellations are not mentioned in the Bible regarding the new creation of the new universe and the new heavens that I have found. In our present-day universe, we are governed by time as Elohim set it up. Genesis 1: 14-19 [14] God (Elohim) said, "Let there be lights in the expanse of sky to divide the day from the night; and let them be for signs, and for seasons, and for days and years; [15] and let them be for lights in the expanse of sky to give light on the earth;" and it was so. [16] God (Elohim) made the two great lights: the greater light to rule the day, and the lesser light to rule the night. He also made the stars. [17] God (Elohim) set them in the expanse of sky to give light to the earth, [18] and to rule over the day and over the night, and to divide the light from the darkness. God (Elohim) saw that it was good. 19 There was evening and there was morning, a fourth day. (WEB) *So in this new creation, will there be the marking of days, weeks, and months? Presently, the Jewish calendar follows the lunar and solar cycles as well as the rotation of the earth. Every new month is marked when the first sliver of light from the moon appears following the New Moon. The New Moon is when the light of the sun does not reflect off of the moon's surface to shine light onto the earth. The Sabbath presently signifies the end of every week, a day to rest from all of one's past week's labors. Just as it was in* Genesis 2: 1-3. 1 The heavens and the earth were finished, and all their vast array. 2 On the seventh day God (Elohim) finished his work which he had made; and he rested on the seventh day from all his work which he had made. 3 God (Elohim) blessed the seventh day, and made it holy, because he rested in it from all his work which he had created and made. (WEB) *Presently, the Sabbath is a time to reflect on all that God has done for us in thankfulness through the whole past week as well as a time to recharge ourselves through resting for the next week. This is in preparation for all that there will be for us to do during the next week. The institution of the Sabbath follows after the pattern of God resting from all the work of creation. However, as we all know, He is still working diligently as the entire Bible shows His endless activities. He didn't sit back, taking an eternal Sabbath, letting things run on their own after creation as some Deists believe. He also doesn't tire out, needing to rest out of exhaustion. He did this to be an example for us in our present state of affairs as we benefit from this rest and time of reflection. Out of His great love and compassion for us, He modeled this as a parent does for a child to imitate. So, this is another element of the new creation to see what will happen and that will be fun to find out if it will continue to exist or not.*

In the new universe everything will be different. For instance, the Periodic Table of Elements that was set up in the first creation will no longer exist. As was mentioned earlier, it is being reiterated. The basic components of the orderly arrangement of the universe, the material elements will have had all their elemental bonds dissolved and rendered void by a great heat. The earth and everything created will be completely incinerated, no longer to be found anywhere, not even its ashes. There will not even be one element or quark left in existence. Newton's Law of Universal Gravitation and Kepler's Laws will be voided. Everything that we understand about how this present-day universe is governed and operates will be obsolete. The totality of existence in the new heavens and earth will be pristine. I understand this is mind-blowing and seemingly incomprehensible. It is somewhat similar to a kindergartener trying to comprehend the complexities of doctorate level physics courses. It is beyond one's understanding. This is alluded to in I Corinthians 2: 6-10. 6 We speak wisdom, however, among those who are full grown, yet a wisdom not of this world nor of the rulers of this world who are coming to nothing. 7 But we speak God's wisdom in a mystery, the wisdom that has been hidden, which God foreordained before the worlds for our glory, 8 which none of the rulers of this world has known. For had they known it, they wouldn't have crucified the Lord of glory. 9 But as it is written, "Things which an eye didn't see, and an ear didn't hear, which didn't enter into the heart of man, these God has prepared for those who love him." 10 But to us, God revealed them through the Spirit. For the Spirit searches all things, yes, the deep things of God. (WEB)

Every person who has ever been conceived in this present creation is eternal. No person will 'disappear' with the eradication of this present creation. The spiritual part of us never ceases to exist, even if it is dead to God, being separated from the abundant life available in God's Kingdom. Thankfully, one's spirit is made alive to eternal existence with God and His blessings through salvation in His only begotten Son, Christ Jesus, as a result of a decision one makes during this present lifetime. Despite the spirit of a person being dead to God by not accepting the free gift of life through salvation in Christ Jesus, it is still eternal. It does not disappear into non-existence. Rather, it is relegated to the Lake of Fire for eternity, separated from God and His love. When Adam sinned, the spiritual part of humanity died to God. It is resurrected and made alive to Elohim through faith in His only Son, Jesus. The eternity of humanity is alluded to in several places throughout the Bible.

Ecclesiastes 12: 1-7, paying particular attention to verse seven where it says the spirit returns to God who gave it. 1 Remember also your Creator in the days of your youth, before the evil days come, and the years draw near, when you will say, "I have no pleasure in them;" 2 Before the sun, the light, the moon, and the stars are darkened, and the clouds return after the rain; 3 in the day when the keepers of the house shall tremble, and the strong men shall bow themselves, and the grinders cease because they are few, and those who look out of the windows are darkened, 4 and the doors shall be shut in the street; when the sound of the grinding is low, and one shall rise up at the voice of a bird, and all the daughters of music shall be brought low; 5 yes, they shall be afraid of heights, and terrors will be on the way; and the almond tree shall blossom, and the grasshopper shall be a burden, and desire shall fail; because man goes to his everlasting home, and the mourners go about the streets; 6 before the silver cord is severed, or the golden bowl is broken, or the pitcher is broken at the spring, or the wheel broken at the cistern, 7 and the dust returns to the earth as it was, and the spirit returns to God who gave it. (WEB)

Daniel 12: 2
2 Many of those who sleep in the dust of the earth will awake, some to everlasting life, and some to shame and everlasting contempt. (WEB)

John 5: 25-29
25 Most certainly I tell you, the hour comes, and now is, when the dead will hear the Son of God's voice; and those who hear will live. 26 For as the Father has life in himself, even so he gave to the Son also to have life in himself. 27 He also gave him authority to execute judgment, because he is a son of man. 28 Don't marvel at this, for the hour comes in which all who are in the tombs will hear his voice 29 and will come out; those who have done good, to the resurrection of life; and those who have done evil, to the resurrection of judgment. (WEB)

II Thessalonians 1: 5-10

5 This is an obvious sign of the righteous judgment of God, to the end that you may be counted worthy of God's Kingdom, for which you also suffer. 6 For it is a righteous thing with God to repay affliction to those who afflict you, 7 and to give relief to you who are afflicted with us when the Lord Jesus is revealed from heaven with his mighty angels in flaming fire, 8 punishing those who don't know God, and to those who don't obey the Good News of our Lord Jesus, 9 who will pay the penalty: eternal destruction from the face of the Lord and from the glory of his might, 10 when he comes in that day to be glorified in his saints and to be admired among all those who have believed, because our testimony to you was believed. (WEB)

If there would ever be a time needed for reflection of the incredible mercy of Yahweh for all of us who love and worship Him, we could go out and look far off toward the Lake of Fire with the souls living without Elohim. If it were not for the incredible mercy of God and our acceptance of His free gift we would be right there with them. During our entire lifetime on earth, God keeps His covenant of love through Jesus' death and resurrection for us. He seeks to bless us, both the righteous and unrighteous. He reaches out to us each and every day. There is not a sin too heinous or repeated too often for Him to turn His back on us, reaching out to us to receive His free gift of salvation. He seeks to bring each one of us to Himself until our very final breath, when the decision for Him or not is finalized. All of our spirits do live forever, either with or without God. Sadly, their spirits in the Lake of Fire are forever alive there. They are those who have rebelled against God, wanting to live their earthly life on their own terms. During their previous lifetime, they refused to acknowledge Him as the Creator of all of Heaven and earth. As a result, they are eternally being eaten by maggots in the ceaseless, unquenchable fire. This is what the second death is, where they are eternally separated from God. This is where they will be consigned. They will be abhorred and seen as loathsome to all of humanity. They were fear-driven of experiencing temporal loss while living their lives on earth, keeping their eyes on what was present around them, ignoring the eternal consequences even when warned. They were unpersuaded to believe in God. Some decided to worship images of their own making, idols that they could control and manage. Many, whether it was actions seen or only in their deepest desires were vile, murderous, sexually immoral by lacking sexual restraint, and liars, being deceitful. They lived in their own illusions, even to the point of using drugs, magical tricks, sorcery, and religious incantations to do this. They tried to manipulate God into giving them more temporal possessions by doing certain things they believed would twist His arm into fulfilling their requests. This even happened during the time of John, the writer of the book of Revelation. During the annual festival of Thargelia the people of Athens and those who came to celebrate would sacrifice either two men or one woman and one man, the ugliest ones they could find or sometimes criminals, as the 'scapegoat' to turn away bad luck or the 'anger of the gods' away from their city. When people turn away from Yahweh, wickedness manifests itself in a variety of ways. We can look around society today and point them out. Thankfully, as Yahweh will have removed all memory of who these people are in relation to us who now exist in the Lake of Fire, there will not be any severe sorrow or desperation felt on our part. Yes, presently, this is beyond our understanding and comprehension. God made each of us as eternal beings. All the angels He made are also eternal beings. The angels who rebelled against God, including Satan will be eternally in the Lake of Fire. All the people that have come into existence are all eternal beings. Therefore, there needs to be a place for every eternal being. Just because God will have created a New Heavens and a New Earth does not mean that those who rejected God and His only Son, Jesus, will be gone with the old heavens and the old earth. They will continue on for eternity. Thus, they need a place for them to be located. That is the reason for the Lake of Fire as that is where they will be 'housed' for eternity, separated from God and His blessings. This is why evangelism and discipleship are so important in the here and now, before they perish into eternal judgment. Again, if you wonder what will happen to those who have never heard of salvation through Jesus Christ, understand that God is just. He cannot and will not do evil by subjecting a person to punishment for something he or she did not do. They will fall under the standard of judgment addressed in Romans chapters one and two. I would recommend doing an in-depth study of these two chapters in Romans if you are truly concerned and want to know the answer. I would recommend beginning your search in two different locations. First, Biblehub. (N.D.). Romans 1:18 Commentaries. Retrieved July 31, 2024, from https://biblehub.com/commentaries/romans/1-18.htm. Second at My Special Place. (2023, March 13). Chuck

Missler - Romans (Session 2) Chapter 1:8-32. Retrieved July 31, 2024, from https://youtu.be/oerszOiyqtg?feature=shared&t=2036 I have referenced this video as beginning at about 34 minutes, though the entire teaching is important. These two locations are referencing skilled commentators on the Bible. They are revered by many as truly understanding and teaching scriptural truths.

Another question that has been considered as well as already somewhat addressed earlier is what about our loved ones? The inquiry is if we will know them in eternity, who they were to us. Wouldn't we be devastated knowing the other loved ones are not with us? I personally believe we will know our loved ones in eternity who are alive in the Lord. I believe the remembrance of our loved ones who were not in the Lord will be erased from memory, similar to our tears being wiped away. What we can conceive of in thought during this present life will not be the same in eternity. First, let's look at the scripture. What will happen during eternity is incomprehensible to us presently as it is alluded to in I Corinthians 2: 9. 9 But as it is written, "Things which an eye didn't see, and an ear didn't hear, which didn't enter into the heart of man, these God has prepared for those who love him." (WEB) *As noted before, this is in conjunction with God wiping away all of our tears as the former ways are no longer, for all things related to evil and suffering are gone. Revelation 21: 3-4* 3 I heard a loud voice out of heaven saying, "Behold, God's dwelling is with people; and he will dwell with them, and they will be his people, and God himself will be with them as their God. 4 He will wipe away every tear from their eyes. Death will be no more; neither will there be mourning, nor crying, nor pain any more. The first things have passed away." (WEB) *There are other scriptures that also allude to our lack of remembrance of the people in our current lives who are not in eternity living life abundantly with us. For instance, Psalm chapter nine talks about the names and remembrance of the cities that rejected God being removed. Psalm 9: 5-8* 5 You (Elyon - Most High) have rebuked the nations. You have destroyed the wicked. You have blotted out their name forever and ever. 6 The enemy is overtaken by endless ruin. The very memory of the cities which you have overthrown has perished. 7 But Yahweh reigns forever. He has prepared his throne for judgment. 8 He will judge the world in righteousness. He will administer judgment to the peoples in uprightness. (WEB) *When Jesus told the people of the interaction of the rich man and Lazarus, the rich man's name was not disclosed, only Lazarus and Abraham. Could it be that the rich man's name had been erased from existence? Luke 16: 19-26* 19 "Now there was a certain rich man, and he was clothed in purple and fine linen, living in luxury every day. 20 A certain beggar, named Lazarus, was taken to his gate, full of sores, 21 and desiring to be fed with the crumbs that fell from the rich man's table. Yes, even the dogs came and licked his sores. 22 The beggar died, and he was carried away by the angels to Abraham's bosom. The rich man also died and was buried. 23 In Hades, he lifted up his eyes, being in torment, and saw Abraham far off, and Lazarus at his bosom. 24 He cried and said, 'Father Abraham, have mercy on me, and send Lazarus, that he may dip the tip of his finger in water and cool my tongue! For I am in anguish in this flame.' 25 "But Abraham said, 'Son, remember that you, in your lifetime, received your good things, and Lazarus, in the same way, bad things. But here he is now comforted and you are in anguish. 26 Besides all this, between us and you there is a great gulf fixed, that those who want to pass from here to you are not able, and that no one may cross over from there to us.' (WEB) *It does not mention that Lazarus saw or spoke to the rich man. It is also interesting that the rich man knew who Abraham and Lazarus were by name. It is implied in scripture that the former evils of this worldly existence will be hidden from us, removed from our memory. This is implied in Isaiah 65: 11-16.* 11 "But you who forsake Yahweh, who forget my holy mountain, who prepare a table for Fortune, and who fill up mixed wine to Destiny; 12 I will destine you to the sword, and you will all bow down to the slaughter; because when I called, you didn't answer. When I spoke, you didn't listen; but you did that which was evil in my eyes, and chose that in which I didn't delight." 13 Therefore the Lord Yahweh says, "Behold, my servants will eat, but you will be hungry; behold, my servants will drink, but you will be thirsty. Behold, my servants will rejoice, but you will be disappointed. 14 Behold, my servants will sing for joy of heart, but you will cry for sorrow of heart, and will wail for anguish of spirit. 15 You will leave your name for a curse to my chosen, and the Lord Yahweh will kill you. He will call his servants by another name, 16 so that he who blesses himself in the earth will bless himself in the God of truth; and he who swears in the earth will swear by the God of truth; because the former troubles are forgotten, and because they are hidden from my eyes. (WEB)

With husbands and wives, I believe we shall know each other, but not in a covenantal marriage relationship. The reason I say this is that Jesus says that there is no marriage in Heaven. I firmly believe we will know each other, just not continuing as husband and wife. To be honest, that makes me a little sad as I dearly love my husband and cannot imagine my life without him. However, I believe we will know who each other are and what our relationship was, but not in the continuation of the marriage relationship. We will as a complete entirety as the Body of Christ be married to Yeshua HaMashiach. This is addressed in Matthew 22: 29-32 and Romans 7: 2-3. Matthew 22: 29-32 29 But Jesus answered them, "You are mistaken, not knowing the Scriptures, nor the power of God. 30 For in the resurrection they neither marry nor are given in marriage, but are like God's angels in heaven. 31 But concerning the resurrection of the dead, haven't you read that which was spoken to you by God, saying, 32 'I am the God of Abraham, and the God of Isaac, and the God of Jacob?' God is not the God of the dead, but of the living." (WEB) *Romans 7: 2-3* 2 For the woman that has a husband is bound by law to the husband while he lives, but if the husband dies, she is discharged from the law of the husband. 3 So then if, while the husband lives, she is joined to another man, she would be called an adulteress. But if the husband dies, she is free from the law, so that she is no adulteress, though she is joined to another man. (WEB)

King David expected to see his infant son again who died during infancy in II Samuel 12: 22-23. 22 He said, "While the child was yet alive, I fasted and wept; for I said, 'Who knows whether Yahweh will not be gracious to me, that the child may live?' 23 But now he is dead. Why should I fast? Can I bring him back again? I will go to him, but he will not return to me." (WEB)

Moses and Elijah were known by Jesus and the three disciples with Him in Matthew 17: 1-4 1 After six days, Jesus took with him Peter, James, and John his brother, and brought them up into a high mountain by themselves. 2 He was changed before them. His face shone like the sun, and his garments became as white as the light. 3 Behold, Moses and Elijah appeared to them talking with him. 4 Peter answered and said to Jesus, "Lord, it is good for us to be here. If you want, let's make three tents here: one for you, one for Moses, and one for Elijah." (WEB) *If they were not known after death, how would Peter have asked Jesus to make tents for them by name? I do not believe Peter ascertained their names by listening in on the conversation and overhearing their names. I believe they were known.*

In I Thessalonians chapter four Paul reminded us for our comfort that we would be together for eternity. If we don't know each other in eternity, then what comfort is there in being back together? It would be a moot point. I Thessalonians 4: 13-18 13 But we don't want you to be ignorant, brothers, concerning those who have fallen asleep, so that you don't grieve like the rest, who have no hope. 14 For if we believe that Jesus died and rose again, even so God will bring with him those who have fallen asleep in Jesus. 15 For this we tell you by the word of the Lord, that we who are alive, who are left until the coming of the Lord, will in no way precede those who have fallen asleep. 16 For the Lord himself will descend from heaven with a shout, with the voice of the archangel and with God's trumpet. The dead in Christ will rise first, 17 then we who are alive, who are left, will be caught up together with them in the clouds to meet the Lord in the air. So we will be with the Lord forever. 18 Therefore comfort one another with these words. (WEB)

All of this can be a difficult subject to talk about as it is beyond our understanding how this can be. Somehow, I believe that we will know our loved ones in the Lord. However, we will not remember our earthly loved ones who are not in the Lord. Their remembrance will be erased from our hearts and minds. I believe there will be people who will know their one parent or child is there, but not feel a loss for the other parent or other child who is not there. One scripture that is always in the back of my mind is Isaiah 54:1. 1 "Sing, barren, you who didn't give birth! Break out into singing, and cry aloud, you who didn't travail with child! For more are the children of the desolate than the children of the married wife," says Yahweh. (WEB) I periodically ponder if those who have never had children will take up those who do not have mothers in eternity with them. As I said, this is presently far beyond our understanding. I am sure there are people who will disagree with me on this. I understand, as this is not explicitly explained in scripture. It might be that we will not remember anything of our earthly existence or people in it. I am only sharing what I believe I see in scripture. We will find out in time.

The Unveiling of New Jerusalem

New Jerusalem, the Holy City of God, that Jesus has been working on for thousands of years will be brought forth to hover over the earth. It will be incredibly beautiful, like a bride that is perfectly prepared for her husband. The home of God will be permanently in the midst of us, His holy people. We will have intimate, unbroken fellowship with Yahweh and He with us. All of this, everything that He has promised is for every child of God. Those who are Yahweh's children are those who hold fast to their faith in Christ Jesus, even unto physical death in this present life. As we are victorious in Christ Jesus and He is in God, He keeps all of us safe in Him. So even in the physical death we experience in our present world as we leave our earthly bodies to go to God we are safely held. We are heirs to all that He has promised. All of the rewards for the work we have done in Christ Jesus are held safely for us, to be brought into eternity for our eternal enjoyment. To each and every person who earnestly desires to drink from the water of eternal life that springs forth from God's presence, Jesus shall freely give it to each person who asks for it. He will always be our precious God and we are His beloved children. How incredibly wonderful this will be!

Isaiah 65: 17-19

17 "For, behold, I create new heavens and a new earth; and the former things shall not be remembered, nor come into mind.

₁₈ But be you glad and rejoice forever in that which I create; for, behold, I create Jerusalem a rejoicing, and her people a joy.
₁₉ I will rejoice in Jerusalem, and joy in my people; and there shall be heard in her no more the voice of weeping and the voice of crying. (WEB)

Isaiah 66: 22-24
₂₂ "For as the new heavens and the new earth, which I will make, shall remain before me," says Yahweh, "so your seed and your name shall remain.
₂₃ It shall happen, that from one new moon to another, and from one Sabbath to another, shall all flesh come to worship before me," says Yahweh.
₂₄ "They shall go forth, and look on the dead bodies of the men who have transgressed against me: for their worm shall not die, neither shall their fire be quenched; and they will be loathsome to all mankind." (WEB)

Revelation 21: 1-8
₁ I saw a new heaven and a new earth: for the first heaven and the first earth have passed away, and the sea (*thalassa - sea or large lake*) is no more. ₂ I saw the holy city, New Jerusalem, coming down out of heaven from God, prepared like a bride adorned for her husband. ₃ I heard a loud voice out of heaven saying, "Behold, God's dwelling is with people, and he will dwell with them, and they will be his people, and God himself will be with them as their God. ₄ He will wipe away from them every tear from their eyes. Death will be no more; neither will there be mourning, nor crying, nor pain, any more. The first things have passed away."
₅ He who sits on the throne said, "Behold, I am making

all things new." He said, "Write, for these words of God are faithful and true." 6 He said to me, "It is done! I am the Alpha and the Omega, the Beginning and the End. I will give freely to him who is thirsty from the spring of the water of life. 7 He who overcomes, I will give him these things. I will be his God, and he will be my son. 8 But for the cowardly, unbelieving, sinners, abominable, murderers, sexually immoral, sorcerers, idolaters, and all liars, their part is in the lake that burns with fire and sulfur, which is the second death." (WEB)

As mentioned earlier, New Jerusalem will be incredible. It will be immense. It is set apart for God in that it is sacred and wrapped in His Shekinah glory. It will shine forth like the brightness of the sun. Its high walls will be clear as crystal, transparent, like pure ice without any impurities. Its foundation will have so many beautiful colors emanating from the precious gems.

The following is a colorful rendition of New Jerusalem's foundations, as it is specifically listed in Revelation. Its entirety is clear as crystal, without any impurities in it, unlike many of these samples.

12. purple or violet, (Amethyst) (2022). Gemselect.com.
https://www.gemselect.com/media/article-images/amethyst-colors_gemselect.jpg

11. orange-red, (*Can also be translated as Jacinth can also be violet.*) (2022). Pinimg.com.
https://i.pinimg.com/originals/ed/99/d0/ed99d0155700fa3b94294d3d6c8a5b00.jpg

10. blue-green or regular green (*Chrysoprasus or Turquoise*) (2022). Shopify.com. https://cdn.shopify.com/s/files/1/0610/6305/files/Turquoise_1024x1024.jpg?5969514462553590154

9. golden-brown-yellow, (*Topaz when pure is clear, but impurities give it colors of pale blue, yellow-orange, orange, green or pink.*) (2015). Navneetgems.com. http://www.navneetgems.com/wp-content/uploads/2015/05/coated-and-irradiated-topaz.jpg

8. clear diamond-like, (*Beryl can be clear like a diamond, but impurities give it color, such as green, yellow or light blue.*) (2022). Gemsociety.org. https://www.gemsociety.org/wp-content/uploads/2013/12/Beryl.jpg

7. yellow-green, or regular green (Chrysolite) (2022). All-Gemstones.com. http://all-gemstones.com/wp-content/uploads/2015/08/chrysolite-stone.jpg

6. pink-red, (*Ruby or Sardine can be translated as red*) (2022). Etsystatic.com. https://i.etsystatic.com/21118310/d/il/fd3bd9/2036795688/il_340x270.2036795688_51q7.jpg?version=0

5. black   (*Onyx, it could also be translated as Sardonyx, which is red.*) (2017). Crystal-Life.com. https://www.crystal-life.com/wp-content/uploads/2016/09/109592-black-onyx-1-14.jpg

4. bluish-green or emerald green (Emerald) (2022). Pinimg.com.
https://i.pinimg.com/originals/d7/ca/0b/d7ca0b46c087783afb9ce52d73d84ebb.jpg

3. brightly multi-colored, (*Chalcedony or Agate could also just be blue*.) (2022). Artprintimages.com.
https://imgc.artprintimages.com/img/print/translucent-mosaic-made-with-slices-of-agate-stone_u-l-q19yxs60.jpg?h=550&p=0&w=550&background=fbfbfb

2. blue (a sapphire blue) (Sapphire) (2022). Withclarity.com.
https://www.withclarity.com/education/user/pages/04.gemstone-education/03.sapphire-gemstone/08.sapphire-value/Blue-Sapphire-Scale-Mobile.jpg

1. multi-colored stripes (*Jasper comes in a variety of colors. It can be a deep red or a green as well as yellow or brown.*) (2022). Naturesexpression.com.
https://www.naturesexpression.com/assets/images/product-images/earth-stone-tiger-eye-jasper-banded.jpg

For more information on the foundation walls, go to For More Study, 9.

Revelation 21: 9-27

9 One of the seven angels who had the seven bowls, who were loaded with the seven last plagues came, and he spoke with me, saying, "Come here. I will show you the wife, the Lamb's bride."

10 He carried me away in the Spirit to a great and high mountain, and showed me the holy city, Jerusalem, coming down out of heaven from God, **11** having the glory (*Shekinah*) of God. Her light was like a most precious stone, as if it was a jasper stone, clear as crystal; **12** having a great and high wall; having twelve gates, and at the gates twelve angels; and names written on them, which are the names of the twelve tribes of the children of Israel. **13** On the east were three gates; and on the north three gates; and on the south three gates; and on the west three gates. **14** The wall of the city had twelve foundations, and on them twelve names of the twelve Apostles of the Lamb. **15** He who spoke with me had for a measure, a golden reed, to measure the city, its gates, and its walls. **16** The city lies foursquare, and its length is as great as its breadth. He measured the city with the reed, Twelve thousand twelve stadia. Its length, breadth, and height are equal. **17** Its wall is one hundred forty-four cubits, by the measure of a man, that is, of an angel. **18** The construction of its wall was jasper. The city was pure gold, like pure glass. **19** The foundations of the city's wall were adorned with all kinds of precious stones. The first foundation was jasper; the second, sapphire; the third, chalcedony; the fourth, emerald; **20** the fifth, sardonyx; the sixth, sardius; the seventh, chrysolite; the eighth, beryl; the ninth, topaz; the tenth, chrysoprasus; the eleventh, jacinth; and the twelfth, amethyst. **21** The twelve gates were twelve pearls. Each one of the gates was made of one pearl.

The street of the city was pure gold, like transparent glass.

22 I saw no temple in it, for the Lord God, the Almighty (*Ruler of the universe*), and the Lamb, are its temple. 23 The city has no need for the sun, neither of the moon, to shine, for the very glory (*Shekinah*) of God illuminated it, and its lamp is the Lamb. 24 The nations will walk in its light. The kings of the earth bring the glory and honor of the nations into it. 25 Its gates will in no way be shut by day (for there will be no night there), 26 and they shall bring the glory and the honor of the nations into it so that they may enter. 27 There will in no way enter into it anything profane, or one who causes an abomination or a lie, but only those who are written in the Lamb's book of life. (WEB)

Inside the Cubed City, New Jerusalem

As one walks up to New Jerusalem, your eyes will first see the magnificence of the twelve foundations and the walls made of jasper. In order to enter New Jerusalem, you will walk through an enormous pearl. Isn't that astounding? A gigantic pearl for each entryway, which is never closed. It is guarded by an angel at each gate. Once you walk through the massive pearl you will see that the city is made of pure gold, so pure, without any impurities, that it is transparent, like glass. The city will not need the sun or moon to light it for the Shekinah glory of God will provide the eternal light throughout it and the Lamb will be like a portable oil-fed lamp, with magnificent light radiating off of Him. The incredible, physical presence of Yahweh will fill the entire place. It will be similar to Revelation chapter four. Revelation 4: 8-11 8 The four living creatures, each one of them having six wings, are full of eyes around and within. They have no rest day and night, saying, "Holy, holy, holy is the Lord God, the Almighty, who was and who is and who is to come!" 9 When the living creatures give glory, honor, and thanks to him who sits on the throne, to him who lives forever and ever, 10 the twenty-four elders fall down before him who sits on the throne and worship him who lives forever and ever, and throw their crowns before the throne, saying, 11 "Worthy are you, our Lord and God, the Holy One, to receive the glory, the honor, and the power, for you created all things, and because of your desire they existed and were created!" (WEB) You may be like me or maybe I am the only person who has ever had a thought like this. To be honest, when I have read these verses in the past, I have thought that it might become monotonous to do this for all eternity. However, in spending time studying and learning more about Adonai, it became quite evident to me that there will never be a time that we will ever completely understand Him. There will never be a 'time' in all of eternity where we will say to each other we have finally learned everything there is to know about God and all that He has for us. We will never have a time where we will say we understand Him fully now and our reason for worshiping Him has come to a conclusion. This is most likely what is happening in Revelation chapter four and all of eternity. Every time they look up at the Lord He reveals to them another aspect of Himself to them or bestows upon them another blessing. As that happens, they fall back down in awe and wonder saying "Holy, holy, holy is the Lord God Almighty!" The incredible love, wonder, awe, mercy, grace, and so much more is mind-blowing. There is no end to learning about and experiencing our God. With this in mind, think about what this place will be like.

As one enters New Jerusalem, there will be an expansive street, a plateia, which is a flat and level broad way, similar to a public square for feasts, celebrations, events, and meeting together. It is also often used as a point of reference when traveling. I wonder if this will be a place where worship groups will spontaneously congregate in New Jerusalem. For instance, throughout earthly history all of the different worship groups and individuals could get together here, taking turns, swapping people as they desire. Worshippers who lived generations before us who are now alive together with us in Heaven can come together and worship right in the physical presence of our Savior and Lord. They could assemble with an endless assortment of instruments and manners of worship coming together in eternity. For instance, King David could join in with many of the different worship groups that we are presently familiar with as desired. Just imagine this. Think about your present-day favorite worship group and picture skilled musicians of the past joining in with them in worship. Also, angels could join in with all of this worship. All of this happening in the physical presence of God. Will the trees there and animals like scripture note them doing, resonate in worshipping God? Will the walls throughout New Jerusalem be emanating worship unto God 24/7? This will be absolutely incredible! Just think of the most powerful, spiritually, and emotionally impacting time of worship you have had in this present life and then multiply it seven times seven. There will not be any temple in the city for the Lord God Almighty and the Lamb are the temple. It is like a marriage, where the husband and wife become one. We, the bride of Christ and Jesus are one. This understanding can blow one's mind. We can end the description of New Jerusalem here, being completely blown away and contented with this alone. However, for there is more to be described. Amazing!

   Down the middle of this street, the plateia, will be a river flowing, which is the water of life. It will be magnificently clear as crystal, flowing from the throne of God and of the Lamb, down the middle of the very large public square. On each side of the river there will be the tree of life, which bears twelve crops of fruit, each month there being a new crop. The leaves from this tree are for the healing of the nations. The curse, katanathema, which dominated the old heavens and *the earth devoting it to destruction, stemming from Adam's sin and possibly the angelic defection prior to Adam, is no longer in existence in the New Heavens and the New Earth. Thus, the Tree of Life is freely available for each and every one of the people of God. Thank you, Jesus, for your incredible mercy and grace!*

As noted previously, the throne of God and of the Lamb will be in this expansive public square area. We will all see His face and His name will be on each of our foreheads. We shall serve the Lord with great joy, because each of us will be specifically qualified to perform sacred services to Him. We will reign forever and ever in fulfillment of what Elohim first created us to do. As Genesis 1:26-27 says: 26 God said, "Let us make man in our image, after our likeness: and let them have dominion (*rule*) over the fish of the sea, and over the birds of the sky, and over the livestock, and over all the earth, and over every creeping thing that creeps on the earth." 27 God created man in his own image. In God's image he created him; male and female he created them. (WEB)

Revelation 22: 1-5
1 He showed me a river of water of life, clear as crystal, proceeding out of the throne of God and of the Lamb, 2 in the middle of its street. On this side of the river and on that was the tree of life, bearing twelve kinds of fruits, yielding its fruit every month. The leaves of the tree were for the healing of the nations (*people joined together with a similar cultural foundation and belief system*). 3 There will be no curse any more. The throne of God and of the Lamb will be in it, and his servants serve him. 4 They will see his

face, and his name will be on their foreheads. 5 There will be no night, and they need no lamp light; for the Lord God will illuminate them. They will reign (*rule, exercise dominion*) forever and ever. (WEB)

The New Jerusalem, The Bride of the Lamb

Hebrews 11: 8-10

8 By faith, Abraham, when he was called, obeyed to go out to the place which he was to receive for an inheritance. He went out, not knowing where he went. 9 By faith, he lived as an alien in the land of promise, as in a land not his own, dwelling in tents, with Isaac and Jacob, the heirs with him of the same promise. 10 For he looked for the city which has the foundations, whose builder and maker is God. (WEB)

Elohim created the first heavens and earth in six days. The second heavens and earth, it does not say specifically, but it appears that He will create them in a day. On the other hand, Jesus told us in John 14: 1-3: 1 "Don't let your heart be troubled. Believe in God. Believe also in me. 2 In my Father's house are many homes. If it weren't so, I would have told you. I am going to prepare a place for you. 3 If I go and prepare a place for you, I will come again, and will receive you to myself; that where I am, you may be there also. (WEB) *The word 'prepare' in the Greek, hetoimazó, means to get everything ready by making the necessary preparations. The word 'room' in the Greek means a permanent place of residence. It is where one lives permanently, which is not left to another or lost. This is part of your permanent inheritance. Jesus left around 33 AD. He has been preparing New Jerusalem for thousands of years. Understand that as He has been preparing it, that He knows each one of us intimately. He knows what we love, what our deepest interests are, what makes us who we are. Each of our abodes He is creating will perfectly match us. In addition to this, all of the rewards we will have gained for the Lord during our earthly lifetimes will be here for us to enjoy for all of eternity. This is described in several scriptures. This first scripture reminds us why our hearts should be on eternity.*

Matthew 6: 19-21
19 "Don't lay up treasures for yourselves on the earth, where moth and rust consume, and where thieves break through and steal; 20 but lay up for yourselves treasures in heaven, where neither moth nor rust consume, and where thieves don't break through and steal; 21 for where your treasure is, there your heart will be also. (WEB)

Revelation 22: 12-13
12 "Behold, I am coming soon! My reward is with me, to repay to each man according to his work. 13 I am the Alpha and the Omega, the First and the Last, the Beginning and the End. (WEB)

Matthew 5: 11-12
11 "Blessed are you when people reproach you, persecute you, and say all kinds of evil against you falsely, for my sake. 12 Rejoice, and be exceedingly glad, for great is your reward in heaven. For that is how they persecuted the prophets who were before you. (WEB)

Luke 6: 22-23, 35
22 Blessed are you when men hate you, and when they exclude and mock you, and throw out your name as evil, for the Son of Man's sake. 23 Rejoice in that day and leap for joy, for behold, your reward is great in

heaven, for their fathers did the same thing to the prophets. ₃₅ But love your enemies, and do good, and lend, expecting nothing back; and your reward will be great, and you will be children of the Most High; for he is kind toward the unthankful and evil. (WEB)

Mark 9: 41
₄₁ For whoever will give you a cup of water to drink in my name because you are Christ's, most certainly I tell you, he will in no way lose his reward. (WEB)

Colossians 3: 23-24
₂₃ And whatever you do, work heartily, as for the Lord and not for men, ₂₄ knowing that from the Lord you will receive the reward of the inheritance; for you serve the Lord Christ. (WEB)

Hebrews 10: 32-36
₃₂ But remember the former days, in which, after you were enlightened, you endured a great struggle with sufferings: ₃₃ partly, being exposed to both reproaches and oppressions, and partly, becoming partakers with those who were treated so. ₃₄ For you both had compassion on me in my chains and joyfully accepted the plundering of your possessions, knowing that you have for yourselves a better possession and an enduring one in the heavens. ₃₅ Therefore don't throw away your boldness, which has a great reward. ₃₆ For you need endurance so that, having done the will of God, you may receive the promise. (WEB)

I Corinthians 3: 10-15
₁₀ According to the grace of God which was given to me, as a wise master builder I laid a foundation, and

another builds on it. But let each man be careful how he builds on it. 11 For no one can lay any other foundation than that which has been laid, which is Jesus Christ. 12 But if anyone builds on the foundation with gold, silver, costly stones, wood, hay, or straw, 13 each man's work will be revealed. For the Day will declare it, because it is revealed in fire; and the fire itself will test what sort of work each man's work is. 14 If any man's work remains which he built on it, he will receive a reward. 15 If any man's work is burned, he will suffer loss, but he himself will be saved, but as through fire. (WEB)

There are also all of the crowns mentioned in the scripture. These are found in II Timothy 4:7-8, James 1:12, I Peter 5:4, and Revelation 2:10. Beyond all of these rewards, Elohim will be physically present with us for all eternity. All of this will be incredible!

Just for very rough estimations the following is the possible amount of space for each person. There could be as little as 1,000 square feet, 93 square meters for each person in which to live up to 14 acres, 5.8 hectares. An explanation of this will be given later.

According to Revelation 21: 15-17, New Jerusalem's walls are at most approximately 1,500 miles, 2,414 kilometers long, wide, and high. Then the thickness of each of the walls are 216 feet, 65.83 meters with a cubit being about 18 inches, 45.72 centimeters. For total width, adding the thickness of both walls together, it would be 432 feet, 131.7 meters. One stadium is a furlong that is the distance of a racetrack; in our measurement being 1/8th of a mile,

0.2 kilometers. 12,000 stadia is approximately 7,920,000 feet, 2,414,016 meters or 1,500 miles, 2,414 kilometers. In air miles, this is approximately from Atlanta, GA to Phoenix, AZ and McAllen, TX to Duluth, MN. Then, of course, one needs to measure the same distance going upwards. Below is a visual example of this:

(2022). Tourofheaven.com. http://tourofheaven.com/images/new-jerusalem/PC140549.jpg and *Size* of New Jerusalem. (n.d.). Tourofheaven.com. Retrieved February 20, 2022, from http://tourofheaven.com/eternal/new-jerusalem/size.aspx

Can you imagine being with John and the unnamed angel measuring this? It was the angel who was holding the measuring rod. The measuring rod was either made of pure gold or overlaid with gold. If it were made purely of gold, it would have been quite heavy. Since the rod would be 10 feet, 3 meters long [decempeda] and maybe 1 inch, 2.5 cm in diameter, it would weigh 60 pounds or 27 kilograms. That would be a long distance to carry this rod. The present day's surveyor's tripod weighs about 15-20 pounds, 7-9 kilograms, just a fraction of this measuring rod. Since one knows the exterior measurement, the inner part of the city minus the thickness of the walls would be 7,919,568 feet, 1,499.9 miles or 2,413,884 meters, 2,413.8 km in each: length, width, and height. The height of New Jerusalem if it were laid on the surface of the present earth would be about 1/167th of the distance to the present moon from the earth, which is 250,000 miles or 402,336 km away. To give another perspective, the highest towering cloud layer is the cumulonimbus, where severe storms originate from these. They can extend from about 700 feet, 200 meters off the ground to almost 70,000 feet, 13 miles, 21,000 meters, 21 kilometers in extreme cases. Therefore, as you look at one of these massive storm clouds, realize New Jerusalem will tower far above these clouds, about one hundred times above these clouds. As of this writing, the tallest building in the world is Burj Khalifa in Dubai. It is 2,722 feet or 829.6 meters tall, almost ½ mile or 0.8 km tall and its core walls are about 2.5 to 4 feet, 500 to 1,300 millimeters thick, depending upon its location. Using man's present-day technology, a building with the height of New Jerusalem would need to have its weight bearing walls about 9,000 feet 2,743 meters wide. Jesus, in His infinite wisdom only needs a fraction of this width to make it structurally sound. Incredible, isn't it? However, this is a moot point as the operational physics and mechanics of our present universe will have been completely removed. All things will be new as previously discussed. Some people believe the measurement in scripture regarding New Jerusalem is actually the perimeter rather than each side. If this measurement is the perimeter rather than each length it would be 1,980,000 feet or 603,504 meters each side, 375 miles or 603.5 km each side, which is around the distance from New York City, New York to Cleveland, Ohio when measured by a straight line.

    This following section of information is extra-biblical using the perimeter as the measurement. Therefore, realize what is written next is only conjecture and imagination, not based on scripture. As there is nothing in scripture that says how many floors there are or the measurements of each floor, it is only done for calculation thoughts. I calculated this out just for a rough understanding of how much space each person might have. To begin with, I did some research on how many people have lived on earth since creation. Creationists believe that as of 2021 there have been approximately 39 billion people who have lived since Adam and Eve. For more information on this, please go to For More Study, 8.

    Now, let's consider if instead of the twelve foundations being at the bottom of the whole city, let us say that there are the twelve foundations throughout the height of the city, one on the bottom, one further up, *another one further beyond that, etcetera. If this were true, here are the calculations for this. Each floor would have a height of 165,000 feet, 50,292 meters, 31.25 miles or 50.3 kilometers. I will explain later what could possibly be on top of each foundation. At this noted height for each level, it is about half of the total present atmospheric level of the earth. The Karman line, which is the measurement from the present Earth's mean sea level to approximately where earth's atmosphere ends, is about 330,000 feet, 100,584 meters. Therefore, each level would be about half of this height. If all 39 billion people were in New Jerusalem, each level would have 3,250,000,000 people on it with each level having 3,920,400,000,000 square feet or 364,217,078,016 square meters. Thus, each person would have 1,206 square feet, 112 square meters in which to live. However, there would be less than this due to walkways or streets and all, but this calculation comes up with an approximation.*

Unfortunately, as scripture says, only a fraction of the total population who have ever lived will accept all that God has provided for us freely in His grace. As scripture says, few are those who are saved. Jesus said this in Matthew 7: 13-14. [13] "Enter in by the narrow gate; for wide is the gate and broad is the way that leads to destruction, and many are those who enter in by it. [14] How narrow is the gate, and restricted is the way that leads to life! Few are those who find it. (WEB) *Also, Luke 13: 22-30 says:* [22] He went on his way through cities and villages, teaching, and traveling on to Jerusalem. [23] One said to him, "Lord, are they few who are saved?" He said to them, [24] "Strive to enter in by the narrow door, for many, I tell you, will seek to enter in, and will not be able. 25 When once the master of the house has risen up, and has shut the door, and you begin to stand outside, and to knock at the door, saying, 'Lord, Lord, open to us!' then he will answer and tell you, 'I don't know you or where you come from.' 26 Then you will begin to say, 'We ate and drank in your presence, and you taught in our streets.' 27 He will say, 'I tell you, I don't know where you come from. Depart from me, all you workers of iniquity.' 28 There will be weeping and gnashing of teeth, when you see Abraham, Isaac, Jacob, and all the prophets, in the Kingdom of God, and yourselves being thrown outside. 29 They will come from the east, west, north, and south, and will sit down in the Kingdom of God. 30 Behold, there are some who are last who will be first, and there are some who are first who will be last." (WEB)

Say for speculation sake that only 40% of all the population of the earth makes it into New Jerusalem. That would mean there will be 15,600,000,000 people living in it. Therefore, on each level there will be 6,310,680 people. This would give each person 2,472 square feet, 230 square meters. This is quite a large house per person. Again, it will be somewhat smaller than this due to walkways or streets, but still quite a large area.

Now, for further postulation, let us consider if there might be 2,472 levels instead of twelve levels. As it does say in Revelation 21:14 that the wall of the city had twelve foundations and the wall of the city in verse 18 was made of jasper. It could be that all twelve foundation layers are at the bottom of the city. Revelation 21:14, 18: 14 The wall of the city had twelve foundations, and on them twelve names of the twelve Apostles of the Lamb. [18] The construction of its wall was jasper... (WEB) *Therefore, all twelve of the foundations may be at the bottom of New Jerusalem. I chose this number 2,472 levels for two reasons. First, it is divisible by twelve, which seems to be a theme throughout New Jerusalem. Second, it allows for each level to be 300 feet or 91.4 meters tall of open area along with a maximum ground depth of 400 feet or 121.9 meters. Then each supporting floor thickness for each level would be 100 feet or 30.5 meters. To be honest, I don't know how a floor could span that length and width without collapsing under its own weight. Maybe there will be load bearing walls or pillars that span all the way from top to bottom as Jesus does speak of pillars and each of us having our own pillar in Revelation 3:12. To be honest, I have no idea as scripture does not say anything about them other than there are pillars in it. However, just as a reiteration, the new heavens and earth will be completely new. What laws of physics govern this world might not govern the new world. Then to be able to possibly aid us in imagining what it might be like, I am going to place some items on the various levels. What I bring up here is probably too limited and small as the creativity of God goes far beyond any of our imaginations. Say such floors I previously calculated could be possible. If so, then Sequoia and Redwood trees could easily fit in each level if so desired with room to spare, including Hyperion, which is the tallest Redwood tree and tallest of any tree world-wide currently living. Apparently, prior to the flood, some trees did grow to be about 900 feet tall. Amazingly, though the Sequoia trees grow to such a great height, their roots only grow down to a depth of*

6-12 feet, 1.8-3.7 meters. They do not have a deep growing tap root, rather their roots wrap around the roots of other Sequoias and trees near to them to remain strong and upright. It's incredible to think that each tree you see is supporting the other trees around them. Another illustration in God's creation that is related to how we, as His people, are all interconnected to each other and to God Himself in order to support each of us and to keep us strong in Him. The Wild Fig Tree from South Africa has the deepest tap root system of 400 feet or 121.9 meters deep. The average tree root depth descends around 20 feet or 6 meters. Having a ground depth of 400 feet, 121.9 meters would also allow for interesting land features. For instance, Lake Erie in the US is around 200 feet or 61 meters deep. This is also more than enough depth that recreational scuba divers normally descend before some toxicity in this present world might occur, just in case scuba diving is something you enjoy and would like to continue in eternity. This height is also more than enough for an avid rock climber to find fulfillment in their pursuits and adventure. Therefore, if there were 2,472 levels with all 39 billion people who have lived since creation were to live in New Jerusalem there would be 15,776,699 people living on each level. With each level having 3,920,400,000,000 square feet or 364,217,078,016 square meters, each person would have 248,493 square feet, 23,086 square meters or 5.7 acres, 2.3 hectares to live, about 498 feet, 151.8 meters in length and 498 feet, 151.8 meters in width, which would be more than enough room for each person. Each person will be blessed by our precious Lord and Savior in filling up our space with what we love to do, bringing us joy.

As noted previously, say for speculation sake that instead of the measurement being the perimeter, rather each measurement is its side in length the following calculations would be possible. Each length, width and height would be 7,919,568 feet, 2,413,884 meters instead of 1,980,000 feet, 603,504 meters for each side. Thus, the space would be much larger, almost four times larger. Then say that only 40% of the population of all who have ever lived on earth are living in it. With the total population being 15,600,000,000, each of the aforementioned levels would have 6,310,680 people. This would give each person 621,232 square feet, 57,714 square meters, 14 acres, 5.8 hectares or .02 square miles to live in; which is quite a large space. I understand these measurements are not exact as several items have not been calculated into the above measurements. For instance, there is the extensive area where everyone congregates together on one of the levels as well as there being necessary ways to get from one place to another, etcetera. These calculations are only done to provide a possible glimpse into what it might be like.

    We are currently seeing through an opaque glass, not allowing us to see through to the other side clearly as illustrated in I Corinthians 13: 12, though this verse is addressing another subject. Also, some people in their perfect eternal location may truly enjoy 'city life' over 'country living.' Personally, I lean more towards country living, thus the reason for my focus on how many acres might be available for each person. Isn't it exciting to try and imagine what it might be like? However one looks at it, it will definitely be beyond where our wildest imagination can take us. New

Jerusalem will be for each one of us the most perfect setting matching our personality and desires that God has instilled in us. As a side note, I understand that the average rancher who has grazing land might need an area over square miles instead of acres. God has not forgotten you and He will have a way to fulfill your desire. More about this will be addressed later. In addition to all that could possibly be inside of New Jerusalem, we will have the incredible pleasure to physically interact with Yahweh daily. There will never be a time that He is physically missing. We will be surrounded by His presence. Furthermore, we will have continual interactions with other believers. There will never again be a time that we will need to say 'goodbye' for years on end as we do now on earth. There will no longer be any more death. On top of all of this, all of our goals and plans which we begin to pursue will be able to be seen through to their completion, watching them come forth step by step to fruition. No more will a goal or project have to be cut off short, left to another generation to fulfill. When completed we may bring them unto Yahweh to show what blessings He has allowed us to fulfill so He and many others may celebrate with us.

This is only a personal note of how my heart cries out for New Jerusalem. However, understand, our view of it is extremely darkened, so we cannot presently see it. In fact, I don't believe we will fully see it in all of its spectacular sights, sounds, smells, taste, or touch until we enter it. Not even during the Millennial Period will we have a true insight into how it will look. The following is my heart's desire I have offered to our Lord. I only share this so that it might prompt you to talk with the Lord about your future with Him. What I have envisioned is most probably miniscule in what our Lord actually has in mind for me. Nevertheless, this is what I imagine. I come up along a road to where Adonai has prepared for me. I will have passed by many other people's spectacular areas on both sides of the road. What exactly the road looks like, I cannot tell. Once I arrive, I see a lush region, full of vegetation and hear beautiful, melodious birds. The scent of the flowers and vegetation gently surrounds me. I see that the land gradually slopes off to a babbling stream below in a valley. Then the land slopes back up overlooking another person's area beyond it. I cannot make out the house at all in my mind. There might be one there. I don't know. However, parts of the land area I am able to picture in my mind. I see there are garden trails meandering peacefully through the food forest. As one walks down the trail, it will disappear behind something, like vegetation or a rock outcropping to reveal a new discovery of fruitful plants and vegetation gracefully filling the area. It is like a series of garden rooms, one after the other, unfolding in their glory and fragrance. There are so many different types of plants throughout the region. I can see such trees as mango, coconut, dates, papaya, black sapote, guava, cacao, persimmon, citrus, stone fruit, pears, and bananas. There are also vines, such as passion fruit, grapes, and dragon fruit. Additionally, there are pineapple, banana yucca and strawberry plants. Beyond all of the areas of fruit, there are other areas, garden rooms, for growing vegetables, herbs, and spices. There is also animal life that adorns the region. Beautiful birds, such as birds of paradise, crested quetzals, hummingbirds, golden pheasants, peacocks, painted buntings, Gouldian finches, and parrots that fly across the sky. They land on the trees and ground. Beyond these birds, you can hear the songs of the Nightingale, Northern Mockingbird, Cuckoo, and American Robin. I can also hear the quiet hum of bees as they fly by to pollinate the flowers throughout the garden. From their hives, honey may safely be collected. There might be a dog or a cat that live there with me, but I am not completely sure. The fruit and vegetables are certainly not all for me. They are for me to share with others, whoever wants them. People may come to the land to pick whatever fruit, vegetables, spices, and/or herbs that they desire. With the harvest they can cook up whatever large dish they desire to share with others. I sort of see a cooking area with a large table and seats surrounded by the garden and of the view below to the valley. People can come from all over to enjoy the food that is cooked up or sumptuous dishes that are created. I am not a gifted cook, so I see others coming with their expertise and creativity to do that and share their culinary masterpieces with others. I also see some people coming just to walk through the garden and eat something that catches their eye. I remember doing that in Austria. I would hike up and down the trails, periodically eating some of the berries that grew next to the trail. What I see in my mind's eye is centralized on having fellowship with one another, with our Lord and His creation. Just as it was in the Garden of Eden, where the original people walked and talked with God. So is this area, a place of communion with Elohim, His creation and each other. Then of course, I will be able to visit with all of the other people in New Jerusalem and on the new earth. I will be able to join in on all of the worship happening as addressed earlier.

Additionally, will Elohim take us on tours of the new universe He has created? Has our Lord put anything in your heart that you are looking forward to in New Jerusalem?

Yahweh has also promised all of us the earth as a place in which we might build houses and inhabit, besides our home in New Jerusalem. Remember my mentioning of ranchers earlier? This is partly addressing this thought. This is shown in Isaiah 65: 17, 21. 17 "For, behold, I create new heavens and a new earth; and the former things shall not be remembered, nor come into mind. 21 They shall build houses, and inhabit them; and they shall plant vineyards, and eat the fruit of them. (WEB) *Since there will no longer be any large bodies of water and seas as Revelation 21:1 explains, rather only rivers and maybe some small lakes or ponds, there will be a lot of land area for people to populate. Furthermore, Revelation 21:24-26 states that all the different ethnicities of God's people will conduct their lives by the brightness of Elohim's Shekinah glory. The leaders of the people on the earth will bring their resources, wealth, and prized items into New Jerusalem. The magnificence of their cities and fertile lands along with their prized items will be brought into New Jerusalem. It appears that God really wants to be involved with and showcase the creativity of His people in order to share and rejoice in the amazing things that His people do, almost like a very proud parent sharing with others what their beloved child has done.*

Revelation 21: 24-26
24 The nations will walk in its light. The kings of the earth bring the glory and honor of the nations into

it. 25 Its gates will in no way be shut by day (*for there will be no night there*), 26 and they shall bring the glory and the honor of the nations into it so that they may enter. (WEB)

Another note on New Jerusalem is in regard to a misunderstanding I had when I was younger. The only reason I bring it up is that maybe there is one other individual out there that is struggling with the same thought I used to ponder so this section might be helpful. Revelation 21:9 to almost the end of the chapter shows us the Bride of Christ, the wife of the Lamb. As I read it, I expected to see people. Instead, what was shown was an enormous building, an inanimate object. Yes, it is an incredible and amazing structure, one that makes anything here on earth seem insignificant in comparison. However, it was immoveable, couldn't speak, couldn't act, create, or do things. It was a structure. I didn't want to be a structure. I was afraid that come the entrance into eternity we, the Body of Christ, would become this inanimate object.

Revelation 21: 9-14
9 One of the seven angels who had the seven bowls, who were loaded with the seven last plagues came, and he spoke with me, saying, "Come here. I will show you the wife, the Lamb's bride."
10 He carried me away in the Spirit to a great and high mountain, and showed me the holy city, Jerusalem, coming down out of heaven from God, 11 having the glory of God. Her light was like a most precious stone, as if it was a jasper stone, clear as crystal; 12 having a great and high wall; having twelve gates, and at the

gates twelve angels; and names written on them, which are the names of the twelve tribes of the children of Israel. 13 On the east were three gates; and on the north three gates; and on the south three gates; and on the west three gates. 14 The wall of the city had twelve foundations, and on them twelve names of the twelve Apostles of the Lamb. (WEB)

When I was young in the Lord and I read this I wondered why we, the Body of Christ, would become an inanimate object. I could not find joy in this. So, I struggled with it while at the same time knowing God knows best and does what is best. I just could not figure out why becoming an inanimate object would be the best for us. As Revelation 3: 12-13 says: 12 He who overcomes, I will make him a pillar in the temple of my God, and he will go out from there no more. I will write on him the name of my God, and the name of the city of my God, the new Jerusalem, which comes down out of heaven from my God, and my own new name. 13 He who has an ear, let him hear what the Spirit says to the assemblies. (WEB) *I tried to find joy in becoming an actual pillar in New Jerusalem, but it was difficult. What helped me finally understand why New Jerusalem is called the Bride of Christ is what happened quite often with the family into which I married. As my husband grew up on a farm, the family would drive out onto the graveled country roads to show me the surrounding areas. As they drove me around they would point out a house or farmland saying, "This is the 'last name' and this other one is the 'last name'." They did not mean that these farmhouses, barns, fields, or croplands were the actual 'last name,' rather these properties seen are where 'last name' live and own or used to live and own. If I had really looked at what it says later in the same chapter and the next, without becoming mentally stuck on the previous verses, I might have seen that it explains New Jerusalem along with the people who come and go from it, living there and those who may not enter it. Only people whose names are written in the Lamb's Book of Life will be allowed to enter it. No one who treats what is godly and sacred as a common thing, or who does what is immoral, or acts deceitfully may even think about entering it. For such people are devoted to destruction, disallowed from being in God's presence. We, who belong to God, His servants, will be freely allowed into His presence as we are qualified to perform sacred services unto Him. We shall see His face and His name will be on our foreheads. We will fulfill the work God gave to mankind in Genesis 1:26 of exercising dominion over all that He has created. We will be active people of God. Revelation 21: 27 and 22:3-5 states:* 27 There will in no way enter into it anything profane, or one who causes an abomination or a lie, but only those who are written in the Lamb's book of life. 3 There will be no curse any more. The throne of God and of the Lamb will be in it, and his servants serve him. 4 They will see his face, and his name will be on their foreheads. 5 There will be no night, and they need no lamp light; for the Lord God will illuminate them. They will reign forever and ever. (WEB) *Therefore, hopefully this has helped anyone who has struggled similarly to me when I was younger about New Jerusalem. Maybe I was the only one who ever thought this. If so, that is fine. I am happy that God helped me in my walk with Him to understand this more clearly. He is so good to each one of us!*

What God Has Said is Truthful and He Loves You

All of God's Words in Revelation are Trustworthy and True

There are at least three witnesses to the writing of the Book of Revelation. As Deuteronomy 19:15b says, 15 *...at the mouth of three witnesses, shall a matter be established.* (WEB) *First, the angel who is the messenger sent directly from Jesus Christ. Second, John, himself, having written all of it and distributed it to the churches. The churches he sent it to are probably the seven churches mentioned in Revelation chapters two and three. A number of them preserved the book of Revelation. Third, Jesus Himself, who has sent this entire message for the Body of Christ. Fourth, what is in Revelation does not contradict what other scripture as a whole says. Fifth, the early churches preserved the book of Revelation and it has been included in the Canon of the Bible. By 180 AD early church leaders saw and accepted all that is in the New Testament as inspired words of God. Over the next two hundred years church councils were convened to make sure only God's true word was included in the Bible. By the late 300s to early 400s AD the New Testament was firmly established, remaining similar to what it was in the 100s AD. Numerous early church fathers have quoted much of what is in our New Testament as being inspired words from God. For example, Clement from 95 AD quotes from eleven New Testament books, including the book of Revelation. Ignatius of Antioch from 107 AD quotes nearly every New Testament book, except some from 3 John. Polycarp was a disciple of the Apostle John who wrote Revelation. He was a pastor over the church in Smyrna. Spanning from the early 100s AD he quotes from all of the New Testament* *books that we have. The books in the New Testament have been used in the early church's sermons and their historically preserved written sermons attest to these books as being God's word. If you would like to do more research on this, please go to For More Study, 10.*

Revelation 22: 6-11
6 He said to me, "These words are faithful (*trustworthy, reliable*) and true (*genuine, truthful*). The Lord God of the spirits of the prophets sent his angel to show to his bondservants the things which must happen soon."
7 "Behold, I come quickly. Blessed is he who keeps the words of the prophecy of this book."
8 Now I, John, am the one who heard and saw these things. When I heard and saw, I fell down to worship before the feet of the angel who had shown me these things. 9 He said to me, "See you don't do it! I am a fellow bondservant with you and with your brothers, the prophets, and with those who keep the words of this book. Worship God."
10 He said to me, "Don't seal up the words of the prophecy of this book, for the time is at hand. 11 He who acts unjustly, let him act unjustly still. He who is filthy, let him be filthy still. He who is righteous, let him do righteousness still. He who is holy, let him be holy still." (WEB)

The word translated 'soon' in Revelation 22:6 and 7 are two different words, related in its root, but having slightly different meanings. τάχει means quickly, speedily, shortly, and then ταχὺ means without any unnecessary delays. In verse six, the words that have been given from God Himself as well as through the angel to John in the book of Revelation show a transition from one point to another as well as show the movement toward this time when the transitions happen. These transitions will speedily take place. Then in verse seven, Jesus promises that His coming will not be put off unnecessarily. He is following God's perfect timetable. When the proverbial clock hits midnight, that exact moment, He is coming. The words in the book of Revelation have been inspired by God. It is He, the Spirit of God, who directs and influences the rational part of mankind granting him or her the power to perceive and grasp eternal concepts. Thus, His words are faithful, reliable, and genuine. We are to keep watch over His words in the book of Revelation and preserve them. His words are not to be sealed up as they were when given to Daniel as the time is now near. We are not to remain silent on what He has revealed to us in His word or conceal it as His return could happen at any time. It could happen during our generation. Come, Lord Jesus!

As the time is so near, Jesus tells all of mankind that those who are set on doing wrong, acting without justice, and doing wickedness to remain doing so. Also, the morally filthy person is to be permitted to remain morally stained with sin and spiritually filthy as all these people's judgment is coming. The people who are set on living uprightly with justice and righteousness, being set apart for God by living differently from the world, are to remain dedicated to God in their life. These people's rewards are coming.

In my own wonderment, if the Lord were to come somewhere between the mid to late 2000s, that would be about 30 generations from the time of Jesus' life on earth. I guess that could be seen as soon. For instance, the following generations are shown in Matthew 1:17. ₁₇ So all the generations from Abraham to David are fourteen generations; and from David to the exile to Babylon fourteen generations; and from the exile to Babylon to the Christ, fourteen generations. (NHEB) *That would be 42 generations from Abraham to Jesus dying on the cross for us. Thus, mid to late 2000s being only 30 generations is less than 42. If it were to be equal to 42 generations, then it would be around the year 2940 and still be seen as soon as it is less time from Adam until Jesus. However, understand, I am not trying to set a date as no one knows the day or the hour. I am just throwing out ideas for pondering the length of generations and what the word 'soon' could be compared to God's timing in the past for understanding the concept.*

Jesus reiterates that He is indeed coming without any unnecessary delays. His reward for each of us who have been saved through His blood will be with Him at His coming. They will be appropriately equal to particular decisions or actions made or done according to the person's whole way of behaving along with one's aims and endeavors in life. I have heard some people in the past ask how King David could be so esteemed by God, called a man after His own heart, when you read in scripture all the bad decisions he made, his poor parenting skills, and the sins in his life. However, God looks at each person's heart, their overall inclination or bent in life. David was humble and would come back to God in repentance each time he sinned. If you read the Psalms that he wrote, you will see his heart's cry in them. He was dependent upon God and quick to return to Him when he strayed from Him and His ways. He is a wonderful example of God's mercy and grace through the blood of Christ Jesus in our humanness. We are not yet perfect in every one of our actions and thoughts in our present state of being. It isn't until our death and resurrection, or rapture, that we will enter the state of perfection and holiness in God, the mortal taking on immortality. There are two different wages, also called rewards, which are coming with Him. The wages of God's blessings obtained through trusting in Yahweh, producing the fruit of righteousness. There is also the wages of punishment obtained through rejecting Yahweh, producing the fruit of wickedness. Jesus is the Originator of all life and He is infinity itself. He is the Eternal One and the remotest one with absolutely nothing beyond Him. He is the very first in rank and the end-goal, the end purpose of all things. He is the Source, the Root as well as the descendant of David. He is the bright Morning Star. Remember what Jesus said to the Church of Thyatira in Revelation 2:26-28. 26 He who overcomes, and he who keeps my works to the end, to him I will give authority over the nations. 27 He will rule them with a rod of iron, shattering them like clay pots; as I also have received of my Father: 28 and I will give him the morning star. (WEB)

II Corinthians 4: 4-6
4 in whom the god of this world has blinded the minds of the unbelieving, that the light of the Good News of the glory of Christ, who is the image of God, should not dawn on them. 5 For we don't preach ourselves, but Christ Jesus as Lord, and ourselves as your

servants for Jesus' sake; 6 seeing it is God who said, "Light will shine out of darkness," who has shone in our hearts, to give the light of the knowledge of the glory of God in the face of Jesus Christ. (WEB)

II Peter 1:19-21
19 We have the more sure word of prophecy; and you do well that you heed it, as to a lamp shining in a dark place, until the day dawns, and the morning star arises in your hearts: 20 knowing this first, that no prophecy of Scripture is of private interpretation. 21 For no prophecy ever came by the will of man: but holy men of God spoke, being moved by the Holy Spirit. (WEB)

The rewards that Jesus has for each one of us who have put our faith and trust in Him are for our blessing. He will extend God's benefits to us, to each one of us who have washed our robes in the blood of Jesus, cleansing them to be white as snow. Our robes, similar to how they were back in Jesus' time, are the outer clothing worn by the upper class. Their outer robe expressed one's character. You knew exactly who that person was by seeing their robe. Revelation 7:13-17 explains who the people in white, long robes are: 13 One of the elders answered, saying to me, "These who are arrayed in white robes, who are they, and from where did they come?" 14 I (*John*) told him, "My lord, you know." He said to me, "These are those who came out of the great tribulation. They washed their robes, and made them white in the Lamb's blood. 15 Therefore they are before the throne of God, they serve him day and night in his temple. He who sits on the throne will spread his tabernacle over them.

₁₆ They will never be hungry, neither thirsty any more; neither will the sun beat on them, nor any heat; ₁₇ for the Lamb who is in the midst of the throne shepherds them, and leads them to springs of waters of life. And God will wipe away every tear from their eyes."
(WEB) *We will have the right as well as the power of choice to decide whenever we want to partake of the fruit of the Tree of Life as well as enter and exit New Jerusalem.*

Those who have not accepted Christ Jesus as their Lord and Savior will be kept outside of all of God's blessings. They are those who produced the fruits of unrighteousness. Jesus lists what the fruit of such people were. Those who had an impure mind, devouring what was not theirs. Those who used drugs in order to live a life of illusion. Those who used magic to manipulate and trick others. Also, those who tried to manipulate God to give them temporary possessions, things that are not eternal. Those who were drawn to various ways of deceiving others through lying or other ways of untruth. People steeped in sexual immorality, such as having sex outside of marriage, adultery, giving their body up for sex in order to receive something in return, as well as a multitude of other sexual sins listed in the Bible, including pornography. Those who have killed someone out of an emotional outburst, for their own personal gain or for any other non-permissible reason. In scripture, there have only been three justifiable reasons that a person may put someone to death. The reasons described have been being part of the military in defense of their country, the end result of a legitimate and legal capital punishment verdict, or self-defense. Another example of one of the fruits of unrighteousness were those who worship an image. This broke the very first commandment of God in Deuteronomy 5:7-10. 7 "You shall have no other gods before me. 8 "You shall not make an engraved image for yourself, [nor] any likeness [of anything] that is in heaven above, or that is in the earth beneath, or that is in the water under the earth: 9 you shall not bow down yourself to them, nor serve them; for I, Yahweh, your God (*Elohim*), am a jealous God (*El Qanna*), visiting the iniquity of the fathers on the children, and on the third and on the fourth generation of those who hate me; 10 and showing loving kindness to thousands of those who love me and keep my commandments. (WEB) *This is why it is so very important that each of us make a choice for Christ Jesus, having become our Lord and Savior during our physical lifetime. He has freely provided the covering of our sin through His blood shed on the cross for us. I pray that each one of you who read this book receive Jesus as your Lord and Savior. I look forward to seeing each one of you in New Jerusalem. As long as you are physically breathing, it is not too late to receive Jesus into your life.*

Epilogue: Invitation and Warning

Revelation 22: 12-19

12 "Behold, I come quickly. My reward is with me, to repay to each man according to his work. 13 I am the Alpha and the Omega, the First and the Last, the Beginning and the End.

14 Blessed are those who do his commandments, that they may have the right to the tree of life, and may enter in by the gates into the city. 15 Outside are the dogs, the sorcerers, the sexually immoral, the murderers, the idolaters, and everyone who loves and practices falsehood.

16 I, Jesus, have sent my angel to testify these things to you for the assemblies. I am the root and the offspring of David; the Bright and Morning Star."

17 The Spirit and the bride say, "Come!" He who hears, let him say, "Come!" He who is thirsty, let him come. He who desires, let him take the water of life freely.

18 I testify to everyone who hears the words of the prophecy of this book, if anyone adds to them, may God add to him the plagues which are written in this book. 19 If anyone takes away from the words of the book of this prophecy, may God take away his part from the tree of life, and out of the holy city, which are written in this book. (WEB)

When I was first saved, accepting Christ Jesus as my Lord and Savior, I began to voraciously read through the entire Bible. I would highlight parts of His word that stood out to me. When I came upon the book of Revelation I saw this warning in verses eighteen and nineteen. Therefore, I decided to not highlight any of the words as I did not want to miss one of them. I knew I had to highlight all of them or none of them at all. The reverence toward God and His word was strong in me and it still is. I do not want to be found adding or omitting any words in the book of Revelation. Through the decades, I have read and listened to numerous sermons, teachings, and commentary on the book of Revelation. I have read reputable commentators on chapter 22:18-19 to help me understand what is meant by omitting and adding words as I wholeheartedly do not want to be found doing either of these acts. Matthew Henry says that those who are condemned in this are those who have corrupted or changed the words of God by adding more to the book of Revelation or taking away from it. Gil's Exposition of the Entire Bible says that to 'add' something does not mean in the writing of a commentary or teaching on it as then the book would not be studied. Rather it is similar to executing the doctrine of the Pharisees. They added layers of traditions of the elders on top of the Law of God. They justified doing this in order to protect the people from transgressing the actual Law of God. Therefore, to break one of the traditions of the elders received the same level of punishment as breaking the actual Law of God. Man's word was put on the same level as God's Word. They broke the words that God said in Deuteronomy 4:1-2. [1] Now, Israel, listen to the statutes and to the ordinances, which I teach you, to do them; that you may live, and go in and possess the land which Yahweh, the God (*Elohim*) of your fathers, gives you. [2] You shall not add to the word which I command you, neither shall you diminish from it, that you may keep the commandments of Yahweh your God (*Elohim*) which I command you. (WEB) *Jesus*

rebuked the Pharisees several times during His ministry for this practice. For instance in Mark 7:6-13: ₆ He (*Jesus*) answered them, "Well did Isaiah prophesy of you hypocrites, as it is written, 'This people honors me with their lips, but their heart is far from me.
₇ But in vain do they worship me, teaching as doctrines the commandments of men.'
₈ "For you set aside the commandment of God, and hold tightly to the tradition of men—the washing of pitchers and cups, and you do many other such things."
₉ He said to them, "Full well do you reject the commandment of God, that you may keep your tradition. ₁₀ For Moses said, 'Honor your father and your mother;' and, 'He who speaks evil of father or mother, let him be put to death.' ₁₁ But you say, 'If a man tells his father or his mother, "Whatever profit you might have received from me is Corban, that is to say, given to God;"' ₁₂ then you no longer allow him to do anything for his father or his mother, ₁₃ making void the word of God by your tradition, which you have handed down. You do many things like this." (WEB)

The Bible as we hold it, God's Word to all of mankind, is complete. There is no more to be added to it. However, in the centuries since the book of Revelation had been written and the Bible completed, people have said to have had visions and revelations from God, which are not seen in the book of Revelation or the rest of the Bible. In response to these occurrences, new religions have been formed from these experiences that contradict and add to God's Word. In addition to this, people put their hope and faith in what people have worked into a church's or denomination's doctrine, putting it on an equal standing with the Word of God. This applies to any religion purporting to be Christian or of God. Unfortunately, they are a compilation of a philosophical mindset, the reasonings of mankind, simply being dreamed up or any number of other things. We all need to be extremely careful to not put mankind's visions, dreams, thinking, reasoning, philosophies, or any other such thing at the same level as God's inspired words, which is the finalized Bible, the complete set of sixty-six books. The safest way for us to interpret the Bible is to allow God's Word in one part of the Bible to interpret other parts of the Bible, looking at it from the perspective of a whole message. Barnes Note on the Bible says those who are condemned are those who have done a few of the following things. First, rejecting what is written in the book of Revelation altogether, looking at it as allegorical or a manmade story. Therefore, they do not put much credence into what has been written and advise people not to read it as it is not understandable. Second, people looking at what is written in the book of Revelation and seeing some of what is written as improbable. Then they omit those words or leave certain sections completely out in the transcription of the book. Third, some person or persons in the future might say that they have received divine revelation from God that needs to be added to the book of Revelation in order to help the church of God further understand what He meant to say, but previously left it out. Unfortunately, most corruptions of God's Word have been done by those who profess some form of Christianity. God gave us the book of Revelation to keep His children, the entire body of Believers, we who trust in Jesus for salvation, forewarned, prepared and ready. He wants every one of us to read it, hear it, and to learn what He has revealed in His Revelation to all of us, through the generations.

For clarification sake, I do want to add that the spiritual gifts of God continue to be alive and active today. I did not mean from what was previously written that God no longer speaks to His people. He does, in many ways. He speaks to them in visions, dreams, through other people, including Christian radio, plus so many other ways. However, what He speaks is not to be added to the Canon of Scripture. What He speaks can be for a number of different reasons. It can be for an individual in a specific situation, the local Body of Christ in the church, or the national Body of Christ in a very specific, present situation. God has not left us alone. He is not like what the Deists advocate He has done after creation. He continues to walk with us and speak with us 24/7. This is explained in many locations throughout the scripture. I Corinthians chapters 12-14 is one such place. If you are unsure about God still being active in our lives or want to learn more about this, use these chapters in I Corinthians as a starting point in your research throughout scripture. Be reassured that He has not left us as orphans.

The Spirit of God and the Bride of Christ say, "Come!" Let the one who earnestly longs for what Christ Jesus has for us, Believers in Him, "Come!" Let the one who is ready and willing to move forward by actively taking hold of the free gift of salvation in Christ Jesus, "Come and freely drink of the water of life."

Jesus, Himself, reiterates that He is indeed coming without any unnecessary delay. This is a truthful statement, which shall come to pass just as He said. Jesus is the Supreme in authority and will always be present to help each one of us, His people. The favor of God, from which all blessings flow is with us. He will never leave or forsake us. This is certainly a truthful statement. Amen!

I began this study as a wonderment of what the signs and possible time period regarding when the rapture might happen. I wanted to know if what is happening in the world around me are the signs of the Tribulation coming soon or not. However, God in His grace not only provided answers to this, but added to it so much more. Not only did He provide answers to my initial question, but also what we as a whole body of Believers are going to experience all the way into eternity. He is so amazing, doing more for us than we even think to ask. Thank you, Lord Jesus! I am so humbled before you, Lord Jesus. I love you and worship you, Jesus! Great and awesome is Your Name for all eternity!

Revelation 22: 20-21
[20] He who testifies (*bears witness*) these things says, "Yes, I come quickly." Amen! Yes, come, Lord Jesus.
[21] The grace of the Lord Jesus Christ be with all the saints. Amen. (WEB)

For More Study

1. *How cubits are measured:*
   - How Long Is a Cubit? (n.d.). Ark Encounter. Retrieved January 16, 2022, from https://arkencounter.com/noahs-ark/cubit/
   - *An enlightening picture that shows the Tabernacle and three different Temples of God over time with size comparison to an American football field.:*
     - (2018). Lorigrimmett.com. Retrieved January 16, 2022, from http://www.lorigrimmett.com/wp-content/uploads/2017/09/End-Times-Temple-Size-Comparison-01-WEB.jpg

2. *Temple side rooms and the open walkway:*
   - Ezekiel 41 Keil and Delitzsch OT Commentary. (n.d.). Biblehub.com. Retrieved January 16, 2022, from https://biblehub.com/commentaries/kad/ezekiel/41.htm

3. *Information on the palm tree in scripture:*
   - The Significance of the Palm Trees. (n.d.). Biblehub.com. Retrieved January 16, 2022, from https://biblehub.com/sermons/auth/clarkson/the_significance_of_the_palm_trees.htm
   - Palm Tree - Encyclopedia of The Bible - Bible Gateway. (n.d.). Www.biblegateway.com. Retrieved January 16, 2022, from https://www.biblegateway.com/resources/encyclopedia-of-the-bible/Palm-Tree

4. *Muslim burial ground on the eastern part of the Temple Mound:*
   Word Press article:
   - n7qvc. (2011, February 17). The Eastern Gate of Jerusalem. N7QVC's Christian Blog. Retrieved January 16, 2022, from https://n7qvc.wordpress.com/2011/02/17/the-eastern-gate-of-jerusalem/

5. *Grain stalks being bundled:*
   - *Grain stalks are bundled and then stood up in the field to completely dry. After a week or two, depending upon the weather, they will be collected to be threshed. Threshing separates the grain heads from the stalk. Winnowing separates the chaff from the edible grain. This is what Jesus' disciples were doing in Luke 6:1-5 as they hungrily walked through the grain field. They were not stealing, rather being provided for according to Leviticus 23:22 -* [22] *"'When you reap the harvest of your land, you shall not wholly reap into the corners of your field, neither shall you gather the gleanings of your harvest: you shall leave them for the poor, and for the foreigner. I am Yahweh your God.'" (WEB)*
   - *For a visual image of bound sheaves of grain shocked together in the field see:*
     - (2022). Dreamstime.com. Retrieved January 16, 2022, from https://thumbs.dreamstime.com/b/sheaves-rye-standing-cornfield-near-cereal-field-42995205.jpg

6. *For an illustration of how the cooking areas, outer court as well as the whole Temple layout will look like, see:*
    - (2022). Messianic-Torah-Truth-Seeker.org. Retrieved January 16, 2022, from https://www.messianic-torah-truth-seeker.org/Torah/Millennial-Temple/Ezek-48.jpg
        - by the Messianic Torah Truth Seeker site:
            - THE GOOD NEWS OF YESHUA - THE LIGHT OF THE WORLD. (n.d.). Messianic-Torah-Truth-Seeker.org. Retrieved January 16, 2022, from https://messianic-torah-truth-seeker.org/

7. *Wadis and Washes: Video examples of these are at these links from around the world:*
    - Buckeye, AZ -
        - Buckeye, AZ Rainbow Wash Flash Flooding - 7/23/2020. (n.d.). Www.youtube.com. Retrieved January 17, 2022, from https://youtu.be/lYvG5z0LqaE
        - *In the US, there are emergency radio and cell phone announcements for potential washes filling up with water as it might be sunny where a person is located on the dry riverbed, but upstream it is raining. The wash fills up and pours downstream. A number of people have died from being caught unexpectedly in a*

> *dry streambed quickly filling up with water.*

- Israel -
  - (LiveLeak) Dangerous flash flood covers dry land in Israel in seconds, Nature Disaster. (n.d.). Www.youtube.com. Retrieved January 17, 2022, from https://youtu.be/6m1lG9FDRiE
- Italy -
  - l'arrivo della piena del Nure a Roncaglia. (n.d.). Www.youtube.com. Retrieved January 17, 2022, from https://youtu.be/xY07U9JXFNw
- Oman -
  - سيل عرمرم الى وادي بني غافر ، لحظات مهيبة لوصول الرستاق ! سلطنة عمان. (n.d.). Www.youtube.com. Retrieved January 17, 2022, from https://youtu.be/ItqbAjLwCtl

8. *38.6 billion people on earth since its creation until 2021:*
   - Wilkin, B. (n.d.). Have Over 100 Billion People Lived on the Earth? – Grace Evangelical Society. Retrieved January 17, 2022, from https://faithalone.org/blog/have-over-100-billion-people-lived-on-the-earth/

9: *All of the colors mentioned in the foundation walls are shown together.*
- (2022). Calvaryportsmouth.co.uk. Retrieved January 17, 2022, from https://www.calvaryportsmouth.co.uk/wp-content/uploads/2016/07/GS12.png
- *This site explains how the colors approximate the Golden Ratio in the color spectrum by Vernon Jenkins:*
  - *Scroll down to "The Twelve Foundation Stones of New Jerusalem"*
  - *37x73.com - THE GOLDEN RATIO. (n.d.). Sites.google.com. Retrieved January 17, 2022, from* https://sites.google.com/site/themathematicalstandard/the-golden-ratio
    - *The wisdom of God goes so far beyond our understanding, even including the seemingly randomness of the colors in the foundation.*
    - *This site is more about Vernon Jenkins. Not that what he has theorized is all infallible. Rather, it is an interesting site to look at to see there is so much more than one can imagine at first glance.*
      - *37x73.com. (n.d.). Sites.google.com. Retrieved January 17, 2022, from* https://sites.google.com/site/themathematicalstandard/home

10. *For more research on how the Bible came into what we have presently:*
    - How We Got the Bible | Bible.org. (n.d.). Bible.org. Retrieved January 17, 2022, from https://bible.org/series/how-we-got-bible

Further Resource for additional study:

Newton's Revised History of Ancient Kingdoms. It was originally published a year after Sir Isaac Newton's death in 1728 by the executor of his estate. The book was still his work in progress. This revised version translates all of the old English, Latin and Greek into modern English to make it understandable. You may find this book on Amazon or any bookstore of your choosing. eBook ISBN: 9780890515563, Hardcover ISBN-13: 9780890515563.

About the Author

She grew up in a Reformed Presbyterian church. In 1978, God reached out to her in a life changing way due to the prayers of many. In 1982, a firm decision to follow after God in salvation was made. In response, God gave her a deep hunger for His Word. She read through the entire Bible in a matter of a few months. From that period onward, she has read through His entire Word countless times with a hunger to learn more about her Savior, Jesus Christ. Through the years, she has been involved in many different churches and ministries; for instance, Baptist, Calvary Chapel, Messianic Congregation, Assembly of God, non-denominational, and home churches. In 1990, she was a missionary in Europe, ministering to persecuted Christians who had been behind the Iron Curtain. Then she was a missionary in Mexico ministering at a school for the deaf. After marrying her beloved husband, they have been serving the Lord together for over thirty years in Alaska and Arizona. She also finds great joy in gardening and learning as much as she can on varied topics of interest.

www.ingramcontent.com/pod-product-compliance
Lightning Source LLC
Chambersburg PA
CBHW070536090426
42735CB00013B/2993